DATE DUE			

BILINGUALISM IN THE UNITED STATES

BILINGUALISM IN THE UNITED STATES

Conflict and Controversy

by Judith Harlan

Franklin Watts
New York London Toronto Sydney
An Impact Book 1991

Photographs Copyright ©: The Bettmann Archive: pp. 14, 20; Comstock Photography: p. 24 (Mike & Carol Werner); UPI/Bettmann Newsphotos: pp. 30, 52, 62: PhotoEdit: pp. 37 (Dave Schaefer), 47 (Felicia Martinez), 110 (Fred Kong); John Blake: p. 43; Paul Conklin: p. 73; Impact Visuals: pp. 80, 96 (both Mark Ludak); Montana State Capital, Office of Public Instruction: p. 84.

Library of Congress Cataloging-in-Publication Data

Harlan, Judith.
Bilingualism in the United States : conflict and controversy / by Judith Harlan.
p.   cm. — (An Impact book)
Includes bibliographical references and index.
Summary: Discusses the politics of bilingual education, recent laws making English the official language in certain states, the movement for a constitutional amendment making English the official language of the United States, and ways in which bilingualism has been handled in other countries.
ISBN 0-531-13001-0
1. Bilingualism—United States—Juvenile literature.   2. Language policy—United States—Juvenile literature.   3. English language—Political aspects—United States—Juvenile literature.
[1. Bilingualism.   2. English language—Political aspects.]
I. Title.
P115.5.U5H37   1991
306.4′46—dc20   91-18518 CIP AC

CONTENTS

For my father, who took me to see the world

1
PIONEERS OF MANY TONGUES

Holá! Konichiwa! Bonjour! The world is a symphony of sounds, where a simple greeting might be *Ne ho, Namaste,* or *yá át ééh?* And a casual "How are you?" could be *Wie gehts? Nalama? Cómo está?* or *Comment ça va?* At least 2,700 different languages make a musical harmony of sound in the world today.[1]

English, however, has established an undisputed place for itself in today's world. It is spoken by at least 750 million people[2] throughout the world. Some estimates put it at one billion people, or about one-fifth of the world's population.[3] And today, say the experts, English is "more widely scattered, more widely spoken and written, than any other language has ever been."[4]

In the United States, English prevails. Over the nation's history, millions of non-English-speaking immigrants and their children have adopted English as their language. Many have forfeited their original languages and forgotten them completely. Many others have held onto their languages and adopted English in addition to their original languages, becoming bilingual.

The United States of America is unique in the world as a country of immigrants—a land that has attracted ambitious people from every region of the globe. All Americans today, with the exception of Native Americans, trace their family history back to an immigrant, to an ancestor who sailed here, walked here, or more recently, flew or drove here, in search of a new way of life. Many of these same Americans also trace their family history back to another language, possibly to a European, African, Asian, or Polynesian one.

In this way, the countries of both North and South America share a history of language that goes back about five hundred years to when an assortment of European explorers began to discover and then to settle these lands. In those early days, when English, French, Portuguese, and Spanish ships all sailed the seas off America's coasts, it was not clear what language would become the language of the newly discovered Americas.

The division of the continents into political nations was still far in the future. The entire two-continent area was simply the Americas. Eventually the United States of America would become the official name of just a *portion* of these Americas. If the colonial leaders of this country—men who understood the political power of words—could have looked far into the future, they might have decided against using the name, the United States of America. But they could not, and did not. So part of the great legacy they left for future generations is a slight inconvenience. United States citizens have no strictly individual national name like Mexican, Canadian, Nicaraguan, or Argentinian to identify themselves as separate from the North and South American continents. They are citizens of the states of America: Americans. The author and editors of this book are sensitive to resistance against the use of *American* to refer solely to the citizens of the United States. But there is no other accepted word of national identity.

Words are the subject of this book: English words, Spanish words, Chinese words. The combination of words, language, is the basis of the issue of bilingualism. Arguments, some of which began before the American Revolution, center on the importance of the English language to the United States. Questions being asked are: Should every American speak English? Does a country need a single language in order to feel unified? Can Americans remain or become united if they speak different languages? Or if they each speak two or three? Is language the glue that holds a country together?

SPANISH-SPEAKING COLONIES

Spanish was one of the first European languages heard in the Western Hemisphere by Native Americans. When they greeted the ships of Christopher Columbus in 1492, the natives of San Salvador spoke to men who sailed for Spain.

Spain, at the time, was master of sea exploration, sharing its dominion not with England or France, but with Portugal. Portugal supported a large inventory of ships and nurtured hopes for discovery of distant wealth and power. In fact, Spain and Portugal held such supreme dominion over sea exploration at the time that they divided the undiscovered portions of the planet between themselves. They envisioned the discovery of new worlds, half of them Spanish, half Portuguese. Portuguese ships, under the countries' joint agreement, got everything east from about 48 degrees west of the Greenwich meridian. Therefore, for the most part, they sailed east, around Africa, looking for trade routes to the Indies. Spanish ships went west, seeking a shorter route to India, as well as spices and precious

11

metals in the newly discovered lands of the Americas.[5]

Spanish was the first European language to gain a foothold in the New World. Columbus led his Spanish sailors around the Caribbean in his voyages from 1493 to 1504. The Spanish explorer Juan Ponce de León sailed the Florida coast in 1513, and Domenico de Pineda explored the Gulf of Mexico from Florida to Cruz (Mexico) in 1519. That was the same year that Ferdinand Magellan set out on a Spanish vessel for humankind's first voyage around the world. About the same time, 1519–1521, Hernando Cortés conquered the Aztecs, waging a brutal invasion that is now viewed as one of the low points of Spain's marches into the New World. In the 1520s, Spanish ships explored the Eastern Seaboard of the United States, from the north of Maine to the tip of Florida. And by 1535, a "tidal wave of inland exploration was underway in South America."[6]

In 1542, Francisco Vásquez de Coronado and his men became the first Europeans to see the Grand Canyon, and also to travel through the Southwest to what is now central Kansas. At about the same time, Hernando de Soto trekked through parts of the U.S. South, from Florida to Tennessee, and west to discover the Mississippi River. Also at the same time, Spanish explorers sailed up the west coast of the continent, into San Diego Bay, and north to Oregon. Finally, in 1565, the Spanish founded America's first permanent European settlement at St. Augustine, Florida.

Through explorers, and later, through missionaries and settlers, Spain brought her language to Mexico, Central and South America, and to the West and Southwest territories of the United States. Under the leadership of Father Junípero Serra, the Spanish established twenty-one missions along the California coast, from San Diego to San Francisco. And the Spaniards set up missions and colonies in Texas and Arizona. All

12

of these were territories that Spain would lose in 1821 to Mexico in the War for Mexican Independence, and Mexico would then lose to the United States in 1848 in the Mexican-American War.

In all of these territories, Spanish was spoken until English-speaking pioneers moved in alongside the Spanish-speaking families. In schools and classrooms in the territory of New Mexico, for example, teachers taught in Spanish as well as in English, even after it passed into American hands[7]. Thus, the history of Spanish in the United States stretches as far back as does the history of English.

ENGLISH-SPEAKING COLONIES

The first English-speaking American settlement that was more than a fort or a stopping-off point for sailors exploring the New World was an English colony at Roanoke, Virginia. In 1587, when this Chesapeake Bay settlement was established, the Spanish regarded this territory as their own. The English established Roanoke partially as an attempt to gain a foothold here, despite Spanish claims.[8] The colonists of Roanoke disappeared, but the English did not give up the idea of planting colonies in America. And in 1607, England's Captain John Smith successfully established Jamestown, and with it brought the English language permanently to America's shores.

The colonial settlements that followed Jamestown differed from each other in many ways. But most of them started with small groups of people banding together to build a life of freedom and profit in the wilderness. In the beginning, they were isolated from one another, separated by miles and miles of dense forest. They developed into different societies, each with its own laws, holidays, and customs. Still, most of the early East Coast settlements were English-speaking communities. A traveler riding up or down the coastal

13

*Dutch traders barter with Indians
on Manhattan island.*

lands toward the end of the 1600s "generally found English the common language, but not much else appeared to unify the people,"[9] says one noted historian.

A few communities, especially the port towns, attracted people who spoke many different languages. The Dutch settlement of New Amsterdam (now New York City) was such a place. A French missionary visiting there in 1643 reported that he heard eighteen languages during his stay. Some of those languages might have been African. The Dutch of New Amsterdam imported kidnapped Africans and enslaved them as domestic servants in their houses.[10]

This particular community was a *polyglot* (multilingual) one. But the majority of the citizens of the original thirteen colonies were English and English-speaking. From the Puritans who sailed in on the *Mayflower* in 1620, to the many English who followed them to settle farther into Massachusetts, to those who settled Charleston, South Carolina, the stamp of English rule and the English language held firm in the east.

In 1790, the year of the first official census count in the United States, the government reported four million Americans, 90 percent of whom descended from English colonists.[11]

EARLY GERMAN-AMERICANS

Some non-English-speaking people attracted attention even in that early stage in the country's history. Two decades before the American Revolution, in 1753, the American patriot and statesman Benjamin Franklin wrote in a letter that he was concerned about the Germans in the colonies. He worried that they were setting up a separate community.

Few of their children in the country know English. They [Germans] import many books from Germany, and of the six printing-houses in the province, two

15

are entirely German, two half-German, half-English and but two entirely English. They have one German newspaper, and one half-German. . . . The signs in our streets have inscriptions in both languages, and in some places only German . . .

In short, unless the stream of their importation could be turned from this to other colonies . . . , they will soon so outnumber us, that all the advantages we have, will, in my opinion, be not able to preserve our language, and even our government will become precarious [fragile]." [12]

True, in parts of Pennsylvania the German language did dominate. In 1766, Germans made up about a third of the population of Pennsylvania. And for the first half of the 1800s, Pennsylvania laws were published in both German and English. [13]

German-Americans, whose numbers continued to grow with increased immigration through the 1800s, presented one of the first language-based controversies in this country. Between 1790 and 1880, Germans made up about 10 percent of America's population, proportionally the largest immigrant group from a single country (aside from the English) that America has ever had at one time. [14]

As American settlers spread westward, the Germans did also, going beyond Pennsylvania into the farmlands of Middle America. In 1840, Germans cast a third of Cincinnati's votes. In that city's schools, teachers taught in both German and English. [15] An 1839 law authorized teachers to speak German, English, or both in the classroom. Milwaukee and St. Louis were home to many Germans, too. In all three cities, the German language was well in evidence, in German newspapers, social and political groups, choirs and bands, as well as in the cities' businesses that by the middle of the 1800s included the beginnings of today's famous breweries.

While coming to America's vast undeveloped lands to start fresh, new lives in a democratic country, Germans were nevertheless determined to maintain their homeland culture. They brought their books, their music, and their philosophies with them. Most lived a bilingual life, participating in the vibrant business life of the United States, while keeping ties to their German ancestry. And, though many thousands of Germans clustered in communities together, they shared their skills and gifts with other Americans. Their language, too, became part of English in America. Many German words, such as semester and seminar, are part of the English language today.[16]

EARLY FRENCH-AMERICANS

The French who settled in America had their influence on the nation, too. French explorers, trappers, traders, and missionaries occupied the seaways of the St. Lawrence and Mississippi rivers. By 1700 they held strategic posts on these rivers and on the Great Lakes. The French also dominated the settlement of New Orleans, creating a unique blend with Spanish settlers and Africans who had been forced to come there as slaves.

When the United States acquired New Orleans and the Louisiana Territory in the 1803 Louisiana Purchase, French was the language of government in New Orleans. It held a place there in all phases of life, alongside English. In fact, when statesmen wrote an act in 1811 to enable Louisiana to draft a constitution and become a state, they had to be very tactful. They did not want to offend French-speaking Louisianans, but at the same time, they did want to guarantee that Louisiana would have an English-speaking government. Therefore, when they wrote the act, they specified that laws passed by Louisiana, as well as records, judicial and legislative proceedings, would be conducted in "the language in which the laws and the judicial and legislative written proceedings of the United States are now published." Without saying the word "English," the act's framers were making sure that Louisiana would conduct its government in English.[17] Louisianans accepted the terms, but they maintained their bilingualism. In 1847, Louisiana passed a law to allow teachers to use French as well as English in their classrooms.[18]

Other language groups have impacted different regions and been part of the great mosaic that became today's United States. Indeed, the list of languages that have been spoken in this nation must include representatives of nearly all the languages of the world. In addition to the Europeans bringing their voices to the East Coast, Asian immigrants brought their languages to the nation. Chinese immigrants helped to settle the West Coast and to build America's railroads, bringing their customs and language with them. Some African languages, Wolof in particular, were sustained for some time in the southern states. The African influence on southern speech is still a disputed topic in the South. But researchers report in *The Story of English* that some of the distinct sounds of southern speech hark back to West African languages.

Native Americans contributed not only to the early settlers' survival, but also gave names to the new plants and animals that they were forced to share with the colonists. Succotash, pecan, persimmon, squash, raccoon, skunk, moose, and chipmunk are all English adaptations of Native American words.

But it has been Spanish that has added the most words to the English language.[19] Lasso, ranch, wrangler, patio, cafeteria, canyon, tornado, vigilantes, and many other western words[20] became part of a cowboy's lingo and then part of the American language as well.

The spread of the English colonies and the English language from America's East Coast to the West and throughout the Southwest is a saga of many forces. Europeans speaking several different languages came to America by the thousands to escape religious persecution in their home countries. And even more of them came to escape poverty and the lack of opportunity at home.

Immigrants stepped off crowded boats and onto the streets of U.S. port cities. As the isolated colonies of the 1700s changed into an established country in the 1800s, many of those immigrants found themselves in New York City. Many settled there, but most traveled to lands beyond the city, many to the farms of the Midwest. And then, when the Midwest was beginning to fill up, newcomers and established Americans as well pushed on farther west, driven by the promise of cheap land, and, in one of the greatest westward rushes of all, gold.

The newcomers arrived on the shores of the United States speaking their native languages, but soon acquired knowledge of English, the language that would help them make a place for themselves in their new country. Some learned to speak English fluently; some forever spoke in heavily accented tones. But for almost all, English was the common language, the one that allowed Swede to chat with Frenchman, Mexican to talk to German, and all people traveling throughout the vast expanses of the country to communicate.

Yet, in the sometimes exciting, sometimes brutal, years of settling the vast area of the United States, many languages were spoken alongside English. Whole communities of German immigrants flourished, as did Swedish settlements, and French and Spanish commu-

19

nities. Neighborhoods within cities held onto their languages and their customs. Language differences were tolerated and bilingualism was the norm for immigrants and their first-generation offspring. Americans added new foreign words to their language on virtually a daily basis, not hesitating to adapt and use words like barbecue (Spanish), stampede (Spanish), sleigh (Dutch), poppycock (Dutch), and levee (French).[21] It seemed in those first years of U.S. history that there would always be enough land, wealth, and, in most cases, even tolerance, to go around.

But as the nineteenth century came to a close and the world entered the twentieth century, things began to change. The United States of America was coming of age. It was no longer a wide-open frontier. In 1869, the country's first transcontinental railway was completed. Farms and ranches were fenced off. Towns were built up. People and goods traveled back and forth from Nebraska to California at an ever-increasing rate. And settlement of the West neared completion.

Before long, instead of encouraging people to come to settle the prairies and plow farms out of the plains, the United States of America began to worry about overcrowded cities, poverty, and crime. And it partially closed its doors.

Immigration laws became stricter, the beginning of what would be a continually increasing strictness

This famous photo by Lewis Hines shows a mother and three children waiting on Ellis Island in New York. The family, having recently arrived from Italy, was concerned about lost baggage.

21

over the next several years. In 1906, Congress passed a law saying that immigrants would have to be able to speak English before they could become citizens.

Meanwhile, a strain of hostility toward people speaking a foreign language on U.S. soil gained great support in the nation. Attacks on foreign languages, such as the one made earlier by Benjamin Franklin against German, became more widespread. Near the end of the nineteenth century, Theodore Roosevelt voiced a common feeling:

> ... the man who becomes completely Americanized ... and who talks United States instead of the dialect of the country which he has of his own free will abandoned, is not only doing his plain duty by his adopted land, but is also rendering to himself a service of immeasurable value.... A man who speaks only German or Swedish may nevertheless be a most useful American citizen; but it is impossible for him to derive the full benefit he should from American citizenship.[22]

Tolerance was on the decline. Anti-German prejudices grew in America, peaking during World War I. In 1915, before the United States entered WWI, about 324,000 students studied German in the United States. By 1922, just a few years later, fewer than 14,000 were enrolled in German classes. And some states, such as Nebraska, outlawed all foreign languages in elementary schools. With anti-German sentiment running high, the town of Findlay, Ohio, imposed a fine of twenty-five dollars on anyone speaking German in the street.[23] And even further, German was forbidden at public meetings or on the telephone.

During WWI, especially, the ability to speak English was taken as a sign of patriotism. Anything foreign was suspicious—the United States was spending lives and energy fighting a war in Europe. In a 1916 speech prior to the war, Theodore Roosevelt said: ". . . unless the immigrant becomes in good faith American and nothing else, then he is out of place in this country and the sooner he leaves it the better."[24]

After the war, however, Americans relaxed again in isolation from the rest of the world. The U.S. Supreme Court struck down antibilingual laws that had been passed by many states during the height of the war. Those laws had banned teaching foreign languages in American schools, and had prohibited teaching *in* foreign languages. The Supreme Court ruled that states could not forbid schools from teaching foreign languages, but it left laws standing in thirty-four states that required that classes other than foreign language classes be taught in English.

But as Americans became more concerned about controlling immigration, English and bilingualism, already an established political issue, became even more of one. "Increasingly," explains one bilingual expert, "the English language was emphasized as a force for civilization and social cohesion [togetherness]."[25] English, it was argued, was the ingredient that made the melting-pot theory work. It was called the common thread, or at other times the glue, that held us all together as Americans.

Over the years, language came up again and again in political discussions. Sometimes the stories of bilingualism were positive, as were the tales of the Navajo language serving as the basis of a military code language during World War II. But other stories were less happy, such as stories of "Spanish detention" in Southwest schools: children kept after school for speaking Spanish on the school grounds.

Finally, in the 1960s, the United States began to embrace the idea of civil rights for all people, including language-minority people. The stage was set for Amer-

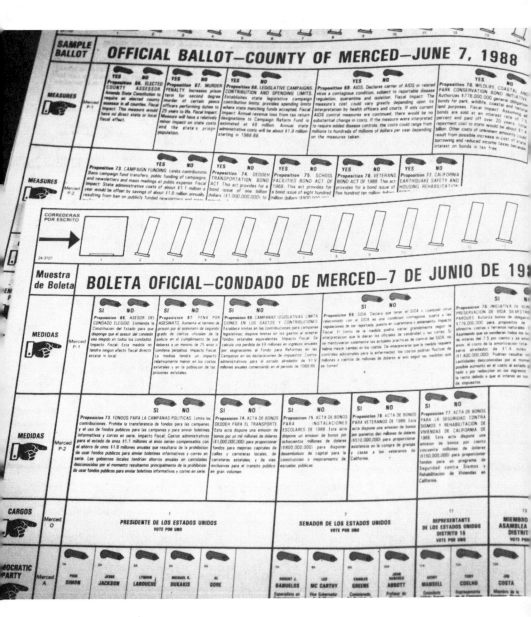

In many areas of the United States, voting ballots are available in both English and Spanish.

icans to consider, once again, their attitudes toward bilingualism. In 1968, Congress passed the Bilingual Education Act, Title VII of the Elementary and Secondary Education Act. This set up a federal fund and allowed schools to compete for funding for bilingual programs.

In 1975, Congress extended the Voting Rights Act, which guaranteed equality at the polls to certain language-minority groups, including Spanish, Asian and Pacific Islanders, Native Americans, and Alaskan Natives and Aleuts. The law said that in certain areas of the United States voting materials must be bilingual, providing information not just in English, but also in these second languages.

By the 1980s, however, opposition to both bilingual education and bilingual voting ballots was growing in some areas of the United States. U.S. English, a group promoting English as the only official language in the nation, led the country in English-only debates. Several other groups lined up in opposition to U.S. English, and the argument reached a high pitch. The 1980s saw several "Official English" laws and state constitutional amendments pass. It also saw many fail. It saw several bills introduced in the U.S. Congress for a national amendment to the Constitution declaring English to be the official language of the country.

Bilingualism in both education and politics was a hot political issue. Emotion and political loyalties ruled as legislators tried to make sense of a fundamental question, the same one Benjamin Franklin seemed to be asking at the country's birth: What role does the English language play in the strength and unity of the United States?

2
BILINGUAL COUNTRIES OF THE WORLD

There is an area—no larger than the U.S.'s New England—along a river that feeds into the Amazon, where Brazil touches up against Colombia, that is home to at least twenty-five separate languages. Most of the people who live there speak at least three of these languages. And they live together quite peacefully. If they do have occasional conflicts, from one language group to the next, it is not over the way they speak.

The individuals in this Amazon region speak several languages chiefly because it is against tribal law to marry a person in the same tribe, and each tribe has its own language. Therefore, every young man courting a young woman learns her language. When she marries him, she moves to his tribe and learns his language. Their children first learn the language of their mother's tribe, and then their father's. The married women in a tribe, who come from many different tribes themselves, pass their languages back and forth to each other. And one language, from the Tukano tribe, is learned by everyone and used as a lingua franca, a common language, when people from different tribes come together.

Interestingly, none of these languages is considered better than any of the others. They all have equal status, and when people gather together they speak whatever language is most convenient for everyone present.

What's so important about this strange Amazon region, says a leading bilingualism expert, is that it shows that "bilingualism is not necessarily related to deep social divisions and conflicts, a fear expressed by many critics of bilingualism."[1] It shows that although citizens in a country *may* fight over language and bilingualism, they also may choose *not* to.

BILINGUAL PARAGUAYANS

Around the world, there are countries that live peacefully while supporting more than one language. There are other countries that fight bitterly over language.

In Paraguay, a country of about 4.5 million people, 90 percent of the population speaks an ancestral Indian language called Guaraní.[2] Most people speak Spanish, too. In fact, says one journalist who has studied the country, "Paraguay today is believed to have the highest degree of national bilingualism in the world."[3]

The Guaraní language is unique in Latin America. "Colonial languages (chiefly Spanish, English, and Portuguese) have long since dominated every other nation in the Hemisphere," explains the journalist, "but Guaraní remains the language of choice, heart, and national identity for [Paraguayans]."[4]

The Guaraní language creates a bridge to the past for all the people of Paraguay, and it is spoken at all levels of society. Still, Spanish is the language used by the government, schools, media, and modern businesses such as banks. Through the years of Paraguay's postcolonial history, Spanish has almost always been

27

the official language of the government. It has held a practical value for any Paraguayan wanting to build a successful business career. And it has held greater social status than has Guaraní.

Until the 1970s, Spanish was the only language used in Paraguayan schools. Pedro Moliñiers, a Guaraní professor and author, remembers being punished for speaking Guaraní during recess when he was a boy. His teacher made him stand for hours with rocks in his hands in front of the class. It was not until 1973 that Paraguay's Ministry of Education changed its Spanish-only rule and allowed Guaraní to be used in bilingual education programs in the schools. And it was still later, in 1987, that the government decided to require all Paraguayan high-school students to study Guaraní.

Paraguayan officials today are aware of the valuable language system they have. Yet, they admit that there are problems with having two languages. The country's bilingual-education programs, in particular, are hotly debated, with some people wanting more use of Guaraní in the classroom and some wanting less.

At the same time, many Paraguayans voice concern over the future of Guaraní. As Paraguay becomes more and more modern, Spanish becomes more important to its citizens. Spanish is the language used in most radio and television programs, and through these broadcasts alone, Paraguayan children and adults are exposed to more Spanish today than in the past. The question is, will this and other modern influences reduce the use of Guaraní in the next generation of Paraguayans? Professor Moliñiers says no, not necessarily. The new emphasis on teaching Guaraní in schools will keep the language alive. Now children will learn to speak it properly and fully, and new words will be added to the language to modernize it. The language will grow with the country.[5]

NATIVE AMERICAN LANGUAGES

Almost every language in the world is more than simply a necessary or practical manner of communicating. Language is an expression of a people's identity and culture. Just as Guaraní has held a place in the lives of Paraguayans through 450 years of Spanish influence, and has remained an expression of their esteem for their history, so too have other languages survived.

Against heavy odds, some Native Americans have held onto their languages. In fact, some 206 different Native American languages are currently spoken in the United States.[6] The languages are a central part of the tribes' cultures, as well as a symbol of their unity.

When Native Americans preserve their languages, they are maintaining a link with their traditions and history. And when they speak in their tribal languages they often express their thoughts in ways uniquely their own. For example, while the sentence, *I am growing corn*, is a quite natural English sentence, in many Indian languages it sounds foolish. In these tribal languages, it is made obvious that the corn is doing the growing, not the gardener.

Some Native American languages, such as Navajo, are spoken fluently and widely in the United States, remaining the first and primary language of many Native Americans. But other languages have had to struggle to stay alive. The Arapaho language on the Wind River Reservation in Wyoming was nearly extinct after World War II. But now young Arapaho students are learning their native language and looking up words in a recently written Arapaho dictionary.

The Oneidas in Wisconsin have also revived their language. Only a few elderly people remained fluent in the Oneida language in the early 1980s. The Oneida district school turned to these elders to help teach young people their traditional language.[7]

An alphabet to standardize the spelling of
Navajo words is shown here with a sentence in
Navajo and the English translation under it.

Different tribes have faced different problems and challenges. Most have come to the conclusion that keeping a language alive is essential for the life of a tribe's culture. But for most, the ability to speak their own tribal language has not been enough. Most Native Americans seek fluency in English, too, partly because English is essential in American business. And Native Americans are striving to improve their economic condition.

MEXICAN INDIAN BILINGUALISM

The Indian population in Mexico faces some of the same well-documented difficulties as do Native Americans in the United States. Mexico is home to almost four million Indians,[8] descendants of ancient tribes. Most of the Indians live in isolated areas and speak their own tribal languages.

"From the beginning of its history," explains Salomón Nahmad Sittón, who was Mexico's director of Indian languages in the early 1980s, "Mexico has been, and continues to be, a country [with many different] cultures and languages."[9]

The Spanish language arrived relatively recently, when Spanish colonizers settled in Mexico, beginning with Cortés's invasions in the early 1500s. Like the settlers in the United States, the Spanish brought their language to their new land, along with their own religion and customs. And, like the Native American tribes, the many different Mexican Indian communities, from their first contact with these Spanish colonizers, "were steadily expelled from their original lands to inaccessible [far away] and inhospitable [difficult] areas,"[10] says Sittón. The Spanish dominated all aspects of life—social, economic, political, and religious.

Over the centuries, the Spanish immigrants and their descendants married into Indian families, until most of Mexico's population became a blend of Spanish

31

and Indian ancestry. But still, chiefly because they were separated from the rest of the country and living in the most "inhospitable" areas, fifty-six groups of Mexico's original Indian nations survive. Most of them live poorly in a poor country. And they face discrimination.

For the past several decades, approximately since 1920, the Mexican government has been trying to bring these isolated Indian groups into closer contact with the greater Mexican society. They have been trying to obtain this goal through education and economic opportunity. They have also been trying to bring the Spanish language into the Indian communities.

"Social scientists, educators, and teachers have been faced with the problem of uniting the nation through common language," explains Sittón. "They have been [looking for methods] to enable almost four million Indians who speak more than fifty languages to use the official language [Spanish], and thereby achieve the goals so anxiously awaited by our nation— unification through a common language."[11]

Through much trial and error, the Mexican government has settled on a program of bilingual education for its Indian citizens. Teachers use the Indians' native language as much as necessary to teach the classes. They teach Spanish, as well, so that their students might become bilingual. But there was a period of time when they taught *only* in Spanish and hoped that the Indian population would, once it spoke Spanish, be absorbed into the greater society in a melting-pot fashion. But that did not work.

"In Mexico people have learned that you cannot stamp out an Indian language,"[12] says Ramón Ruiz, a University of California professor. Bilingualism, however, is a goal they hope can be achieved.

CANADA'S EPIC LANGUAGE STRUGGLES

While Mexico, the United States' neighbor to the south, has been grappling with its long-term bilingual issues, the U.S.'s northern neighbor, Canada, has been going through a bilingual crisis. In Canada, French and English are languages in conflict.

In late 1989, Lise and Pierre Belcourt, parents of four young children in Ontario, Canada, tried to explain the situation that French-speaking Canadians found themselves in. Their own native language was French, although they were bilingual in English, the Belcourts explained. They wanted their children to speak French, too. But they were surrounded by English. At home, the Belcourts could tune their television to a French station, and could read French stories to the children at night. But once the children went to school, they would learn English. And in their community, English-speaking people outnumbered French-speakers five to one. How long would it be, the Belcourts worried, before their children started speaking English all the time and forgot their French?

The ability to speak French is important, explained Lise Belcourt, because it is the family's connection to its heritage of French tradition. "It is not only a question of language. It is a question of feeling and culture,"[13] she said.

Both English and French have a long history in Canada. French trappers and settlers were the first to come to Canada, and they brought their French language with them to the frontier. The English came after the French, settling alongside them. The differences between the French and the English settlers were obvious even from the beginning. The French were Catholic and they set up their communities in the French system of landlord ownership. They brought the French culture and Catholic religion with them, and tried to maintain a civilization that mirrored the one they had left behind.

The English did the same. And in England at the time there was a long-standing feeling of animosity toward the French. England and France had often been at war and had always been rivals. The English had also been at odds with the Roman Catholic Church for two hundred years. In England, no Roman Catholic was allowed to hold public office or even to be an officer in the country's army or navy.

The English settlers and French settlers of Canada, with their mutual prejudices and suspicions, were destined to conflict.

The French held onto Canada until 1763, when they lost it to England under the Treaty of Paris. English rule took over Canada, but both the English and the French would have to make compromises if they were to live there peacefully, side by side. And they did.

England, though taking possession of the territories, allowed the French language and culture to hold onto its place in Canadian life. And through the years, as Canada's vast lands were settled and explored, a few areas, especially in Quebec, continued to be dominated by Canadians of a French-Catholic heritage.

The majority of Canada's landmass, however, was from then on settled by English and other, non-French, pioneers. The English language soon dominated in Canada. In most areas, French became a minority language.

In some areas, French and English existed together peacefully. In others, French-speaking settlers met discrimination. Still, the French language remained an official language. In 1867, when the British North America Act created the Canadian federation, which, with amendments, is today's Canadian constitution, the country's bilingual policy continued. The act specified that both languages would be official in Canada. Both would have equal standing in legislative and judicial proceedings at both the Canadian and Quebec levels. (The province of Quebec was singled out because it is the one province where French-speaking Canadians are the majority.)

What began in Canada's early years as a difference in religion, culture, and language became in later years a severe political division. The French language and its speakers were sometimes treated with tolerance, sometimes with intolerance. In 1864, for example, French-speaking Acadians in Nova Scotia were told they could no longer have separate, French, Catholic schools. In 1871, New Brunswick outlawed the teaching of French and in French. And in 1877, French was outlawed on Prince Edward Island.[14]

Quebec developed into the French section of Canada. And the tug-of-war between English-speaking and French-speaking provinces continued. In 1915, the province of Manitoba banned bilingual teaching in its schools, and other provinces did the same.[15] During World Wars I and II, when Canada joined the Allies and fought as part of the British Commonwealth, many French Canadians resisted. They resented the fact, explains one Canadian journalist, "that they, a minority within Canada, were drawn into war by the English-speaking and British-descended majority."[16]

The idea that the French-speaking province of Quebec was "a distinct [unique and separate] part of Canada" gained ground. Many Quebecois began to demand a separate status and separate privileges within the Canadian confederation. At the same time, many English-speaking Canadians sent up a cry for "one language, one school, one flag."[17]

The fragile unity of French-speaking and English-speaking Canadians seemed to be coming apart. By the 1960s, Canadian leaders agreed that drastic action was necessary to hold things together and to keep Quebec from breaking away from the rest of the nation. Official bilingualism appeared to be the solution to the nation's problems.

Prime Minister Pierre Trudeau, a Quebecois himself, led the nation in setting up a new bilingual policy.

One of the effects of the policy was to require many government employees to become bilingual. A percentage of the Royal Canadian Mounted Police, the Canadian armed forces, and the staff of federally owned businesses such as Air Canada had to speak both French and English.

After the bilingual law passed, Canadians saw many small, and some large, changes in their communities. Canadians telephoning into federal government offices were greeted with receptionists saying, "Good morning, *bonjour.*" Drivers began to see road signs in both English and French. And English-speaking children were encouraged to enroll in French classes to increase their chances for future employment in bilingual Canada.

True bilingualism has never really been achieved for most Canadians, however, despite the government's official bilingual policy. Only 7 percent of Canada's native English speakers are bilingual in French, and only about 46 percent of Canada's French speakers are bilingual in English. Even in Quebec, only about 45 percent of English-speaking residents speak French, and only about 38 percent of French-speaking residents speak English.[18] Consequently, though Canada is bilingual, most Canadians are not.

The Canadian government's policy of bilingualism, moreover, has not yet pulled the country together as was hoped. In 1980, Quebec held a vote on whether or not it wanted independence from Canada. Quebecois voted against leaving Canada, but the tension between Quebec and the other Canadian provinces did not go away. The two sides bickered over their languages through their political institutions. In December 1988, Quebec passed a bill outlawing the use of English on outdoor signs. All signs would have to be in French.[19]

Many signs are printed in both English and French in "bilingual" Canada.

Also in 1988, Quebec supported a groundbreaking trade agreement with the United States. The agreement would open the doors to trade between Canada and the United States, and would remove many of the protections both nations had in place. The French-speaking Quebec province stood alone in its support of the agreement. Most Canadians from the other, English-speaking provinces opposed the agreement and feared that it would hurt their businesses.

While the debates over the trade agreement with the United States raged, Canada was also trying to agree on important constitutional amendments. The amendments, written in 1987, were called the Meech Lake Accord. The deadline for all the ten provinces to sign the amendments was June 1990. But as the deadline neared, Canadians remained locked in battle over one of the items in the accord—Quebec's demands for special status as a "distinct society" within the Canadian confederation. The special status would guarantee that Quebec could make its own, separate laws about language.

Since Quebec had already passed a law that banned English on outdoor signs, opponents worried that it might become more French-only if it had the constitutional right to do so. What's more, the Meech Lake Accord also strengthened bilingualism in Canada as a whole, by including it in the amendments.

Canadians grew further and further apart during the Meech Lake Accord arguments; thus the amendments which had been intended to unite the country divided it instead.

In February 1990, a town of 113,000 people in Ontario declared itself to be English-only. Twenty-seven other city governments in Ontario had already passed English-only laws.[20] And organizations dedicated to establishing English as Canada's one language added new members to their rosters.

In June 1990, the Meech Lake Accord failed. It did not win the votes in the provinces that it needed to become law. Of course, the debate did not end there. It continues, as French- and English-speaking Canadians try to solve centuries-old disagreements.

OTHER COUNTRIES, MANY LANGUAGES

In many countries around the world, citizens work with the challenge of having more than one language. Some are succeeding. Some are failing. A few examples of both:

In 1975, Peru tried to establish bilingualism. It named Quechua, an Indian language, as one of its official languages, with Spanish as the other. Quechua maintained its official status for four years until the government changed hands. Then Quechua and another Indian language, Aymara, were reclassified as languages that *could* be used officially. But Spanish is the only declared official Peruvian language, and the Indian languages are not being widely used outside of Indian communities. Bilingual education so far has not been successful in Peru.[21]

In Wales, both the Welsh language and culture survive. Welsh has official equality with English, is taught in the schools along with English, and road signs are bilingual.[22] About 20 percent of Wales's population of almost 3 million people is bilingual, and 32,000 speak only Welsh.[23]

Sweden attracted a million immigrants from Yugoslavia, Greece, and Turkey after World War II. It is also home to a large population of Finland natives. The country supports a wide range of bilingual education programs for its various inhabitants.[24]

In the Soviet Union, during the historic changes of 1989 and 1990, when the Berlin Wall came down and the Soviet East Bloc countries struggled to decide their new, independent futures, language came under discussion. Bilingualism in Russian and the countries' home languages had been the Soviet policy in Eastern Europe. But Russian was never a well-loved language. "Russian was forced on us," one student said.

When the East Bloc countries gained new freedoms, one of the first things many students did was quit studying Russian. They did not, however, give up their bilingualism. In order to maintain contact with the rest of the world and to become economically competitive, the countries' students sought out German and English teachers. Polish students leaned toward bilingualism in English and Polish. Young Hungarians seemed to be favoring English as their second language, too. But German seemed to be winning favor in Czechoslovakia. The question was not *whether* to be bilingual, but in which language to be bilingual.[25]

Switzerland, meanwhile, is a quadrilingual country, home to four languages: German, French, Italian, and Romansh. As of 1980, most Swiss nationals spoke German (73.5 percent). The next most popular language, French, was spoken by 20.1 percent of the Swiss. Italian was spoken by 4.5 percent of the citizens, and Romansh by almost 1 percent. The rest spoke a variety of languages. Switzerland has long been known for its neutral stance in politics. Its citizens are admired for their bilingual abilities.[26]

Many reasons and forces drive countries to be bilingual. They may establish bilingual societies for economic reasons, such as do the people in East European countries. They may be bilingual for cultural reasons, as are the people of Wales, Paraguay, Canada, and in those unusual territories on the Amazon. In almost all cases, decisions have to be made about the importance of language in people's lives. And the importance of language in a country's economic life must also be decided by its people. The United States is not alone in its debates over English and the possibilities of bilingualism.

40

3

· WHY ARGUE OVER LANGUAGE?

In June 1990, the University of Northern Colorado ignited a heated debate over bilingualism when it invited a conservative Republican and former president of U.S. English to be its graduation day speaker. The proposed speaker, Linda Chavez, was a strong supporter of Official English legislation. Many students at the university and leaders of the League of United Latin American Citizens (LULAC) objected loudly to allowing Chavez to speak at the graduation ceremony.

"Having her here is like having Phyllis Schlafly [the lawyer and political activist who led the fight against other women for the Equal Rights Amendment] speak on women's rights," said one university student.

Chavez responded to criticism from the students and the Hispanic community by accusing them of "McCarthyism," referring to Senator Joseph McCarthy, the senator who led a nationwide anti-Communist witch hunt in the early 1950s.[1]

Accusations flew back and forth between Chavez

and the university students. The local newspapers got involved, with editorials for both sides. University officials, after listening to the arguments, changed their minds and canceled their invitation to Chavez, replacing her with another speaker for the graduation day ceremonies. Chavez accused the university of taking away her right to free speech. Students picketed outside a building when she showed up for another, separate, speech at another Colorado university. They accused her of deserting her own fellow Hispanics and of promoting *xenophobia* (fear and hatred of strangers or foreigners).

The issue of whether or not Chavez should speak at the university's graduation ceremonies became both emotional and political. Some said that this was *not* a freedom-of-speech issue. Graduation day speeches are by invitation only. They are not meant to be political platforms. Therefore, Chavez should accept her rejection and come back to the university and debate the issue at another, more appropriate, time. In fact, she was invited back for a debate, and the university then found a different graduation day speaker—one who did not represent a political position.

FIGHTING WORDS

Calm voices do not usually prevail in the emotionally charged atmosphere of English language vs. bilingualism debates. Accusations of racism and xenophobia are launched by one side. Accusations of arrogance and unreasonableness are launched by the other.

But before a discussion of the debate begins, a few important terms must be understood. These are: Official English, English-Only, bilingualism, and English Plus.

"Official English" is the phrase preferred by supporters of legislation who seek to make English the official language of a region, state, or of the United States.

42

*Although the invitation to Linda Chavez to speak
at the University of Northern Colorado's graduation
ceremony was withdrawn, Ms. Chavez
did talk at the university's diversity conference in
September 1990.*

Those against English-language legislation will often use the term "English-Only" in talking about this same legislation because the word *only* suggests that the laws seek to exclude any languages other than English.

"Bilingualism" is used as a catchall term in general debates, usually meaning any situation in which languages in addition to English are used, either beside English or in place of it.

"English Plus" is a term used chiefly by those who support bilingual causes. "Plus" refers to learning English in *addition* to any other native language, encouraging fluency in both languages.

STIRRING UP THE MELTING POT

At the bottom of the debate over language is a fundamental disagreement about the makeup of the U.S. population. The United States as a nation has always been proud of saying it is a land of immigrants. All U.S. citizens, except Native Americans, are either from another country themselves or are descended from someone who is. American society, as a result of these many different peoples, is a multicultured, multiethnic, multireligious one. And multivoiced. Yet it is one that was built originally on European immigration. Even today, the U.S. Bureau of the Census lists "White" Americans as being about 80 percent of the country's population. African-Americans make up just over 10 percent. Asians and Pacific Islanders make up less than 3 percent of Americans. And Hispanics as of 1988 were listed as under 10 percent.[2]

Within each of these groups are several different groups: A list of Asians includes Koreans, Chinese, Vietnamese, Cambodians, and many others; a list of Hispanics includes Mexicans, Puerto Ricans, Cubans, Spaniards, Argentinians, Nicaraguans, Salvadorans, Peruvians, and others, each with their own cultural histories. Today, politicians argue over how closely con-

44

nected these and the rest of the many different peoples and voices in America need to be. They ask, should people strive to be similarly "American"? That is, should they "melt" into the pot originally created by European immigrants? Or, can they maintain their cultural differences and be American, too? Can we all be different but equally respected ingredients in an American "salad"?

Those who support a melting-pot theory point with concern to the large communities in the nation where a second language is spoken. One writer tries to explain the concern that he felt when he realized how numerous the Spanish-speaking population in the United States is:

> *It was a sunny day late in June, and crowds of people were milling about on the streets of New York, where I live. There was nothing special going on, no fiesta, no protest, no ethnic promotion. The car cards on my subway train, advertising everything from Eastern Airlines to Preparation-H in Spanish may have started me thinking, I don't know. But walking up Fifth Avenue toward my dentist's office, I felt concern (okay, fear)—abruptly, it seemed—as I noticed I was hearing Spanish voices everywhere and realized that I had been hearing them in shops, hotels, and restaurants all over the city. It was as though New York had achieved a kind of Hispanic critical mass. Nothing in particular jarred me. I just noticed, felt surrounded by strangers and, for an anxious moment, like Rip Van Winkle in my own hometown.* [3]

What this writer describes, and what is at the heart of the argument for Official English laws in this country, is his alarm at the "differentness" and changes that surround him. This writer is concerned about the extent of Spanish use, and he's concerned that in the future Hispanics (along with other minority Americans) and Anglos could become divided. His voice, in comparison to many in the debate, is a thoughtful voice, with a moderate and even a caring tone.

At the same time, his story describes the cultural shock many English-speaking Americans feel when they enter sections of town where another language dominates.

"We feel we're being squeezed out," said a woman in a city near Los Angeles that has become dominated by Spanish-speaking residents. "I went shopping downtown looking for an English [recording] to give for a gift," she added. "I couldn't find one. I was so mad I wanted to move."[4]

In her town of Huntington Park, Hispanics make up more than 90 percent of the population of 59,000. In the early 1960s, the story at Huntington Park was almost exactly opposite to what it is today: then 80 percent of its population was Anglo.

The changes in the community have been dramatic. But not everyone sees the new community as the "heartbreaking" area that some of the older residents describe it to be. To many of the new, Hispanic immigrants, the area feels comforting.

One Spanish-speaking resident describes how it feels to him. "I go to the library and most of the people speak Spanish. . . . In the parks, in the streets, there are people with the same values. It feels good."[5] And Pacific Boulevard, a street of shops that had been doing poorly in the 1970s, is today a bustling Hispanic business district that its patrons call *La Calle*. Street vendors sell corn on the cob and burritos to strolling Latino shoppers. *Zapaterías* sell shoes. *Tiendas* sell clothing. Music drifts out from the open doors of Mexican restaurants. *La Calle* has the feel and look of a successful business district.

Spanish signs are common in business areas with a concentrated Hispanic population.

U.S. English, formed in 1983 to promote English as the official language of the United States, looks at this community and others like it with great anxiety. Former Senator S.I. Hayakawa, one of the founders of U.S. English, refers to "the real danger that is peculiarly the problem of a nation of immigrants." He quotes President Theodore Roosevelt as saying, "The one absolutely certain way of bringing this nation to ruin, of preventing all possibility of its continuing to be a nation at all, would be to permit it to become a tangle of squabbling nationalities."[6]

Unity is the goal of Official English legislation, say members of U.S. English and others who support the legislation. They point to communities such as Huntington Park, California, as examples of communities that are falling apart along language lines.

They remind listeners that the United States, as they see it, has traditionally been a melting pot. Immigrants have come to America and purposefully cast off the languages and traditions of their native countries. Stories in American history books celebrate the immigrants who started life fresh in the New World, adopted American foods, American holidays, and American words.

To U.S. English and its followers, it seems that today's newcomers are not casting off their old loyalties. They're not changing into Americans. And one of the most noticeable things they are not changing is their language. They are asking monolingual (one-language) Americans to accept a bilingual society.

One Official English advocate explains that "bilingualism undermines the very basis on which this country has been built: assimilation of diverse nationalities into a new nationality."[7]

"What is new today," reports the *National Review*, "is a political program of de-assimilation: the assertion [statement] that newcomers have nothing to learn about the society they wish to join and that the necessity of learning is, in fact, an infringement [violation] of their rights."[8] The statement implies that today's immigrants are refusing to join American society and are instead setting up their own separate communities.

TOSSING A NEW SALAD

Supporters of bilingualism vehemently deny that neighborhoods are resisting assimilation or that they are rejecting American values.

"Although we are a nation of immigrants, we have had a love-hate relationship with our diverse cultural heritage," explain two Hispanic leaders, Paul Cejas, a cofounder of SALAD, the Spanish American League Against Discrimination, and Rosa Castro Feinberg, a Dade County, Florida, school board member.

Throughout our history, they continue, Americans have clung to a belief in the melting-pot assimilationist theory. But "in reality, the melting pot idea only applied to the Anglo and Western European, not so much to the Southern and Eastern European. The racially and ethnically different—blacks, Orientals, American Indians and Hispanics—have been filtered out of the melting pot for more than 200 years."[9] Thus, Hispanics and other language-minority groups have always been to some extent separate from the mainstream.

Another speaker on behalf of an American "salad," James Stalker, also points out that, on the positive side, maintaining cultural differences has always been part of the American life-style. "We are all immigrants," he says, . . . "[and] we expect others to be tolerant and accepting of our Scots, Polish, Russian, or African heritage."[10] We expect to be able to celebrate and maintain these ancestral ties. Shouldn't we in turn be accepting of others' heritages?

The picture of a salad of Americans works to some degree when looking at history. But it works especially well in understanding today's changing United States. Throughout the nineteenth century, most U.S. immigrants came from Europe. They mixed in relatively easily with the country's previous European immigrants. But during this century, although many Europeans came to the United States, especially during the two world wars, more and more of the country's immigrants have come from Asia and from Hispanic countries south of the U.S. border. In 1988, more than 80 percent of all the immigrants coming to the United States legally that year came from Mexico, Central and South America, the Caribbean, and Asia.

Wars and political disruptions in different parts of the world have also sent Hispanic and Asian refugees to the United States by the thousands. According to the U.S. Bureau of the Census, between 1961 and 1980, after Fidel Castro took over Cuba, more than 473,000 Cubans came to the United States of America. And running from their war-torn country, more than 425,000 Vietnamese came here between 1971 and 1988.

When experts predict what the United States will be like in the twenty-first century, they talk about "the browning of America." Because of immigration patterns and birthrates, white Americans, they predict, will be a minority in this country by the middle of the next century. "By 2056," writes one journalist, "when someone born today will be sixty-six years old, the 'average' U.S. resident . . . will trace his or her descent to Africa, Asia, the Hispanic world, the Pacific Islands, Arabia—almost anywhere but white Europe."[11]

America's new immigrants bring new cultures with them that are different from today's majority population. The people are noticeable because their faces are brown and their features are different from the old Anglo and European faces and features that dominate in America. But as people, and as immigrants, they come to the United States for the same reasons that people from around the world have always come to this country. They come for freedom and opportunity.

They come because they are individuals in search of personal goals. They are independent enough to leave their homelands, and this independence makes them similar to other Americans. Independence is a vital part of American culture, tradition, and history—individual independence is a cherished American trait! Though different in their backgrounds, tastes, languages, and cultures, most of America's new immigrants reflect that American spirit of independence and go-getting ambition in the celebrated tradition of immigrants to this country.

Cejas and Feinberg are optimistic that the United States can become more tolerant and accepting of these new American immigrants. ". . . In post-civil-rights America, we are fast approaching the goal of becoming a nation where the many are making a more perfect union, a union that looks more like a full salad bowl than a melting pot lacking essential ingredients,"[12] they say.

SALAD and English Plus support the idea of a plural approach to society. Pluralism, though not exactly opposite to assimilation, rejects the idea that immigrants must assimilate into a melting pot. Pluralism believes that many different cultures can live side by side in harmony. The cultures lend flavor to each other and influence each other, but they do not disappear. The "salad" image of America is a pluralism image. The "salad bowl approach wants to add fresh, ongoing sustenance to the health and vigor that strengthen our proud heritage of diversity,"[13] say Cejas and Feinberg.

Some of the strength and vigor brought by new immigrants to America are most noticeable in a city like Miami, Florida, which has been revived by Cubans. It's visible in a city like Huntington Park, whose *La*

51

*A group of 3,200 people representing 106 countries
are sworn in as United States citizens. During
a single week in November 1985, a record 39,000
people became citizens in Los Angeles.*

Calle has become a prospering center of business. Or it's visible in the many Japanese-Americans who have held onto their language and now can work with American companies in building markets in Asia. So, while Official English campaigners worry that Americans are too different from each other, and that Americans speak too many languages, English Plus advocates celebrate America's multicultural community.

SOCIAL GLUE OR DANGEROUS QUICKSAND?

Official English supporters argue that the English language is a major element that holds American communities together. Language differences fragment a population, they say. They maintain that people who speak different languages set up separate neighborhoods that can't communicate with one another and therefore become isolated.

"English, our common language, is the social glue that holds this multicultural country together, making all of us, regardless of national origin, Americans,"[14] says one Official English advocate.

"Adopting the English language has always been part of becoming American," says another. "Relative ease of communication in a single language has provided a kind of national glue, a common thread to the creation and development of a nation that is spread over a wide area and harbors diverse interests, beliefs and national origins."[15]

The English language, if everyone is forced to use it, would have a unifying power, say Official English supporters.

Bilingual and English Plus supporters agree that English is important for Americans and that it is part of the American culture. But they argue that it is not the best or only social glue that Americans have. The forces that unite Americans go much deeper than the language we speak, they argue. Language is an accident of birth. English-speaking Americans, Spanish-speaking Americans, immigrant Americans who speak their original languages, and Native Americans who speak their languages, are all equally American.

Far more important than language in uniting Americans is the American sense of shared destiny. The freedoms and opportunities that attract people from all over the world to the United States unite us all, they explain. The belief in individual rights, freedoms, and constitutional protections, government's and society's tolerance for people who are culturally different, or who believe in a different religion from the mainstream, all unite us as Americans. Our independent-spirited democracy and our free economy also unite us all as Americans.[16]

Americans are more than just a group of people who live near each other and speak the same language. Americans share a culture. It's an adopted culture for many immigrants. It's an elastic culture that allows for much individual expression. It is, at bottom, a culture of shared ideas and dreams.

And the best social glue in the United States of America is shared opportunities.

QUEBEC IN AMERICA

Despite any and all arguments, Official English advocates still see bilingualism as a danger to political unity. For examples of how divided a bilingual society can be, they point to other countries that have accepted bilingualism. And, especially, they call on Americans to study what has happened in Canada, a country that has lived with friction between its English-speaking citizens and its French-speaking citizens throughout its history. (See chapter 2.)

"I have experienced the problems in Canada caused by an officially bilingual government," S.I. Hayakawa writes in a letter asking for donations to U.S.

English. Hayakawa, a man of Japanese heritage, was born in Canada. "That's why [because of firsthand knowledge] I devoted so much of my time and resources to helping America avoid the turmoil of a nation divided by a language barrier."[17]

Another supporter for the Official English cause described Canada as "a chillingly instructive example of how bilingualism can work in a very practical way to distort and disrupt a country."[18]

Bilingual advocates do not agree with Hayakawa or with other antibilingual speakers who warn that the United States could become like Canada. Canada's problems, they explain, "do not stem from the use of one language or another. The real issue is political dominance of one group over another."[19]

Canada's dispute between English- and French-speaking citizens has roots in the divisions between its early French and English settlers. The dispute has been fueled through many divisive historical events that through the years have pushed the two sides further apart. Today, French-speaking Quebec citizens, certainly, are united to each other and separated from English-Canadians by language and culture. But the country is divided, too, by the political and economic divisions between French and English Canadians. The French language in Canada supplys a symbol of the division between French- and English-speaking Canadians.

Language has likewise been used in many political arguments in the history of America. When Benjamin Franklin expressed deep concern over being "germanized" by the Germans in colonial America, he was using language as the focus of his arguments. But his real concern, says a language-history expert, was the threat that the German community would not support his choice for colonial governor. It was the political unity of the Germans that worried Franklin. He worried that they would all vote together against his candidate.

*   *   *

Throughout American history, when language has been, as it was with Benjamin Franklin, the focus of debate, the real issue has not been language itself, say some historians. Language has simply become "a focus of arguments made for political, social, or economic purpose."[20]

Language is a "symbol," or a "signal,"[21] says one Hispanic leader. And in today's Official English debates, it masks the real fears, concerns, and goals of Official English advocates, one of those fears being the fear of change. But change is coming. And as communities in the United States change, political power will become increasingly more equally shared among all Americans. As each year passes, more seats of political power are sought by Asians and Hispanics, seats that once were the undisputed property of Anglo-Americans, and, more recently, of African-Americans. A hard lesson in sharing is being learned by all Americans, majority and minority, in the process.

But Americans are also learning that there are more factors than simply language or heritage that determine how individual citizens vote and therefore how they wield their political power. Income and education heavily influence all voters—Hispanic, Asian, African-American, Anglo-American, and others. Any political block that might grow out of the minority community, then, has to be one based on many more issues than simply language.

As Linda Chavez's dismissal from the University of Northern Colorado's graduation ceremonies illustrates, Hispanics do not all think alike. In fact, they do not all agree on bilingualism. Neither do all Asian-Americans. One of the founders of U.S. English, after all, is a Japanese-American, S.I. Hayakawa. And daily newspapers provide coverage of minority-language leaders divided on bilingual and other political issues.

56

Bilingual leaders voice alarm over Official English trends in the U.S. Some note a "mean spiritedness"[22] in demands for English only. Others see the symbol of language being used to mask fears of uncontrollable immigration.

"Clearly," says Martha Jiminez, spokesperson for MALDEF (Mexican-American Legal Defense and Educational Fund), Official English campaigns are attempts "to keep [Asians and Hispanics] out,"[23] and to close immigration opportunities to them.

The Official English campaign is, in fact, "an anti-immigration statement,"[24] says Kathryn Imahara, director of the Language Rights Program at the Asian-Pacific American Legal Center.

U.S. English spokesperson Stanley Diamond denies that his organization's Official English campaign is anti-immigration. Official English laws are simply a "powerful message," he says. They send "a message to immigrants that in order to function here, you must be able to speak, read, and write English."[25]

One University of Pennsylvania sociolinguist told *Newsweek* magazine, however, that in some cases the arguments over language are, indeed, "a real cover for bigotry. . . . It's easier to say we're afraid of English being overwhelmed than to say we don't want any more [minorities] around here."[26]

Official English advocates argue that they are not promoting bigotry. Indeed, they say, they are promoting greater tolerance. Promoting Official English "is a way to eliminate [racism and prejudice]," says one author. As people from many lands assimilate into American culture and speak English, prejudices "dissolve into distant memories."[27]

BILINGUAL COUNTRY OR BILINGUAL PEOPLE?

Confusion develops on both sides of the Official English issue over exactly what bilingualism means. Does bilingualism mean two languages for the United States? Or two languages for Americans? There is a difference.

Official English advocates fear that bilingualism really means two separate languages. In other words, the country itself could be bilingual, but the American people would not be. Some Americans would speak only Spanish, for example. Others would speak only English. Only a few Americans would speak English and Spanish. Most Americans, then, would still be monolingual, but they would be living in a bilingual country, and they would be separated into their own separate-language neighborhoods.

English Plus advocates define bilingualism differently. Not the country, but Americans themselves, could be bilingual, they say. Spanish-speaking Americans would also speak English. English-speaking Americans would also speak Spanish or another language. Bilingualism would be encouraged among all Americans. Other languages would have the same respect as the English language, and bilingual citizens would help the United States in its international businesses. This would be an English Plus approach to language.

"From an international point of view, it is foolish not to develop the human resource of bilingualism," says Antonia Hernandez, a Hispanic activist. "The world is 'getting smaller.' We need to relate to other countries and other cultures on a much more sophisticated level."[28]

The many citizens in the United States who speak a foreign language first and English second could be a valuable resource for American corporations wanting to sell their products in another country. Japanese-Americans might help the United States become more competitive in the Japanese market. Chinese-Americans could represent U.S. business in China.

Hispanic-Americans could open doors to markets throughout Central and South America. The United States' immigrant heritage could be an enormous advantage in embassies and corporations throughout the world. But instead, says one language expert, second-language Americans are considered more of a problem than an asset.

English Plus advocates would like to see mutual respect between English and other languages. And almost all bilingual advocates would like to see the debate over language separated from the underlying political and emotional motives that drive it.

Yet the debate over language continues. And it continues to be emotional and political. In the 1980s and into the 1990s, Official English advocates won several victories in the U.S. political arena, convincing voters and legislators to pass English-language laws and constitutional amendments at the state level.

4
THE POLITICS OF OFFICIAL ENGLISH LAWS TODAY

It takes only a few words to stir up the fires of debate over language. As an example, take the following words from a 1989 proposed amendment to the United States Constitution:

> *SECTION 1. The English language shall be the official language of the United States.*
> *SECTION 2. The Congress shall have the power to enforce this article by appropriate legislation.*

These few words have been fought over in debate after debate across the nation.

Speaking in favor of the amendment, Representative Norman D. Shumway (R-CA), says, "A single language in government, a common language, greatly enhances national unity, political stability, social equality and economic efficiency."[1]

Speaking against the amendment, Arturo Madrid, a Hispanic leader, says, "Attempts to impose English on the U.S. population have served historically to divide the nation. . . . A sane national language policy would . . . promote multilingualism."[2]

"If such an amendment were to pass it would be the first time that the Constitution was used to *take away* individual rights, rather than to extend or strengthen them," adds Antonia Hernandez, an Hispanic leader. "Never in our history, except during the brief period of Prohibition [when liquor was outlawed in the United States], has the amendment process been used to revoke [take back] basic rights."[3]

The introduction of the English Language Amendment did not start in a vacuum. Language has been a hotly debated issue for several years. The 1970s, following the 1968 passage of the Bilingual Education Act, proved to be a decade of concern for bilingual matters, a decade when hopes were high. Goals were set for bilingual education. The federal government allocated money in its budget for it. And the presidents holding office, both Gerald Ford and Jimmy Carter, supported liberal bilingual-education programs.

But Ronald Reagan's 1980 election signaled a change in policy. Bilingual-education programs were challenged. And the focus of language debates shifted to include Official English legislation. Laws prohibiting languages other than English were introduced in state legislatures. Amendments to state constitutions were proposed and so were statewide propositions.

Before the 1980s, only two states in the nation had laws stating that English was their official language. Nebraska had a constitutional amendment, passed in 1923, making English its official language. Illinois had a 1923 law on its books declaring English to be its official language. Hawaii had two official languages, English and Hawaiian. But then the 1980s began.

In 1980, voters in Dade County, Florida, approved an antibilingual ordinance. It made it illegal to spend

61

Ronald Reagan's election to U.S. president made a big difference in the government stand on bilingual education. Here, President Jimmy Carter (left) and the president-elect pose with their wives before heading to the inauguration ceremony.

public money on the use of any language other than English. Spanish-language marriage ceremonies were halted; Spanish-language public transportation signs were taken down.

In 1981, the legislature in Virginia declared English its official state language and made English the language of instruction in public schools.

In 1983, San Francisco voters passed a proposition calling for a return to English-only voting ballots in the city.

In 1984, Indiana and Kentucky legislatures passed declarations making English their official state language. Tennessee passed a similar law, and also outlawed any language but English in official documents, communications, and voting ballots, and it made English the language of instruction in its public schools. California voters approved a proposition calling for an end to bilingual ballots throughout the state.

(In the same year, however, in a move contrary to Official English moves in other states, the state of New York decided to require all students to study a foreign language, and it started giving foreign language credit to nonnative English speakers.)

In 1986, California voters passed Proposition 63, making English the official language of the state. And Georgia passed a resolution declaring English their state language.

In 1987, Official English measures were considered in thirty-seven states. The measures passed in five states: Arkansas, Mississippi, North Carolina, South Carolina, and North Dakota.

In 1988, English-language amendments passed in Arizona, Colorado, and Florida.

In 1989, the Official English campaign was temporarily slowed down. And three states, New Mexico, Washington, and Oregon, approved English Plus policies.[4] These policies are the opposite of Official English amendments and legislation. Instead of restricting the government to the use of English, they give official respect and recognition to languages learned in addition to English. They welcome different cultures and encourage the use of any language in business, government, and private affairs.[5]

In 1990, the Official English movement gained momentum again. And Alabama passed an Official English constitutional amendment with a stunning 89.6 percent of the vote from Alabamans.

And for 1991, U.S. English was targeting four more states for Official English legislation—Montana, Missouri, West Virginia, and Utah.[6]

THE FEDERAL ENGLISH LANGUAGE AMENDMENT

At the same time as the states around the country in the 1980s were forming their Official English laws, members of Congress in Washington, D.C., were debating a national Official English policy.

In the congressional session of 1981 to 1982, Senator S. I. Hayakawa (R-CA) introduced a resolution asking for an amendment to the United States Constitution. He wanted English declared the official language of the United States, and he wanted to prohibit all levels of government from using any other language. Congress did not act on his resolution, and it died.

In the Congress of 1983 to 1984, Congressman Norman D. Shumway (R-CA), introduced an English Language Amendment (ELA) in the House of Representatives. Senator Walter Huddleston (R-KY) introduced one in the Senate. A Senate subcommittee held hearings to discuss the issue.

In the Congress of 1985 to 1986, Senator Steven D. Symms (R-ID) introduced an ELA. Senator James A. McClure (R-ID) introduced a resolution expressing that the "Sense of Congress" is that English is the official language of the United States. The two senators combined forces and tried to get English as an official language written into a new immigration law that was then being discussed. They failed.

In the Congress of 1987 to 1988, a half-dozen new versions of an ELA were introduced on Capitol Hill. All were discussed, but no decisions were reached.

In the Congress of 1989 to 1990, several bills, some carried over from the previous Congress and some new ones, were seriously discussed.[7]

As the nation moved into the last decade of the twentieth century, the debate over the English language was far from over. Official English advocates continued to work at the state and federal levels to push for amendments and laws declaring English the only official language of the land. Minority-language groups, meanwhile, continued to argue against the legislation, and to seek new ways to teach English to minorities and to open up doors to opportunity for minority-language Americans. The two sides squared off, neither side ready to give in to the other.

ORGANIZATIONS FOR AND AGAINST

On the side supporting English language amendments, the leading organization is U.S. English. This group describes itself as a national, nonprofit organization of 350,000 members, founded in 1983. "U.S. English promotes maintenance of the traditional role of English as the common language of the United States," the organization's fact sheets stated.

To promote the English language, U.S. English supports legislation, both at state and federal levels, that declares English the official language. The group's goals include restricting the language on voting ballots and government documents to English only. They also want to reform bilingual-education programs to promote those that get students out of second-language

65

and into English-only classrooms quickly. The group believed that languages other than English should be limited to private life—the home, church, business.

U.S. English lists several famous and highly respected Americans on its advisory board, but it also faced public scandal in 1988 when one of its office memos was made public. The memo, written by one of the group's founders, Dr. John Tanton, expressed views that some said were anti-Hispanic. Linda Chavez, a Hispanic who was serving as the organization's president at the time the memo surfaced (and who later was the center of a graduation day dispute in Colorado [see chapter 3]), called Tanton's comments "repugnant . . . not excusable . . . anti-Hispanic and anti-Catholic."[8] Chavez quit the organization, and Tanton resigned also.

U.S. English, recovering from the scandal, continued to be the most vocal organization supporting English language amendments in 1989 and 1990.

On the side opposing English language amendments are several ethnic, language, and civil rights organizations. An umbrella group for many of these organizations is EPIC, the English Plus Information Clearinghouse. EPIC was established in 1987. Included in the list of organizations that helped found and endorse EPIC are: the American Civil Liberties Union, the American Jewish Committee, the Mexican-American Legal Defense and Educational Fund (MALDEF), the National Puerto Rican Coalition, the National Council of Teachers of English, the League of United Latin American Citizens, and many others.[9]

EPIC members support the English Plus concept. They want opportunities for Americans to learn English well, and also to master a second language. English will remain the primary language in the United States, they say. But Official English amendments divide the nation. It is better, they say, and wiser in today's world economy, to encourage fluency in two or more languages than it is to encourage monolingualism.

English-language laws create an environment, or a climate, that starts everyone questioning everything said and done in languages other than English, say English Plus leaders. People look at Korean-language store signs and wonder, possibly for the first time, whether these are legal. They look at bilingual warning signs near danger zones or in hospitals and wonder, are these legal? They look at rule books on driving and question, are these legal? They're in an elevator and they hear one person tell another to quit speaking Spanish because English is now the state language. And they don't know, is this legal now? Language laws have created confusion, say English Plus leaders. They relate the stories that came into their offices after passage of English-Only laws in Arizona, Colorado, and Florida:

A cashier in a Coral Gables Publix supermarket was overheard asking a coworker a question in Spanish. It was the day after Florida's English language amendment passed. The store manager suspended the clerk for ten days without pay, because Florida had become an Official English state.

In a Colorado incident, a school-bus driver ordered children to stop speaking Spanish because Colorado had passed an Official English amendment and he thought other languages were no longer allowed.

In Denver, Colorado, a South American customer in a fast-food restaurant didn't understand the menu and asked an employee to translate. The employee started to, but the manager, reminding him of Colorado's English-Only law, stopped him.

In Arizona, after voters approved an Official English amendment, the prisons' Board of Pardons and

Paroles postponed hearings for non-English-speaking prisoners until the confusion was cleared up over whether or not they could speak a language other than English during their hearings.[10]

Since California passed its English language amendment, "there has been a rash of English-Only workplace rules,"[11] says Edward Chen, an attorney for MALDEF.

Another attorney, Kathryn Imahara, as mentioned earlier, the director of the Language Rights Program at the Asian-Pacific American Legal Center, relates the story of one of her clients, Tony Wong. He worked for a life insurance company in Los Angeles. One morning when he came to work he found an interoffice memo in his in box. At first he thought it was a joke. It said, "Communication by any other language (aside from English) is prohibited and is grounds for probation and termination."

When Wong realized the memo was not a joke, he said, it "felt like a slap in the face."[12] He and coworkers sometimes spoke Chinese during breaks, he said, but never in front of clients. They felt the memo was an insult.

The passage of the California law, relates Imahara, resulted in many workplace rules such as those that Tony Wong faced. Yet, such rules in California—even with the Official English amendment—are legal only if the employer has "a very, very, very good reason" for setting the rules. Only three reasons are considered good enough, says Imahara. An employer can require English in (1) situations such as surgery where everyone must communicate closely to protect the safety of the patient; (2) hazardous jobs such as oil drilling, where teams must communicate well for the safety of the workers; and (3) customer-oriented businesses such as stores, where employers can require that workers speak English to English-speaking customers.[13]

Tony Wong was able to file a complaint against his employer because his employer did not have any of these three very good reasons for requiring his employees to only speak English. Wong's attorneys argued that the Civil Rights Act of 1964 protects citizens against workplace discrimination on the basis of national origin, among other things. And language, under U.S. Equal Employment Opportunity Commission guidelines, is seen as such an important part of a person's national origin that the two can't be separated. Therefore, Wong's attorneys claimed, forbidding him to speak his language on the job was national-origin discrimination.

Other California employees have filed language discrimination complaints with the Equal Employment Opportunity Commission. And others still are involved in lawsuits over forbidden languages. In the cases that MALDEF has been involved in, the organization's attorneys say, almost every business has revoked or changed its English-Only rules. It's almost as if the companies' managers didn't realize that the English-Only rules they were making were discriminatory. "People are sensitized to blatant racist remarks," says Kathryn Imahara. "They know [they are] not acceptable. [But] language issues are somehow divorced from that."[14]

While bilingual advocates point out the problems that English-language laws have brought on, U.S. English supporters relate some incidents that they feel show that English-language laws are needed.

In El Paso, Texas, in 1989, U.S. English reported, a road crew worker sued El Paso County because no one would speak English to him. His supervisor and coworkers, he said, not only refused to speak English to him, but they also discriminated against him because he was not Hispanic.

In Miami, two English-speaking women filed complaints against a cleaning service. The company would not hire them because they could not speak Spanish, they said.

U.S. English also reported that an Official English law was needed because there have been incidents of government officials speaking languages other than English at public meetings. They point to a 1988 public hearing in Los Angeles over whether to build a new prison in a Hispanic part of town. City Councilwoman Gloria Molina spoke in Spanish, instead of English, at the hearing. And at a 1987 Arizona Pima County Council meeting, Vice-Chairman David Yetman also chose to speak in Spanish.

These incidents all work together to show that "the traditional role of English is being challenged,"[15] says U.S. English. To meet that challenge, U.S. English would really like a United States constitutional amendment.

An English language amendment to the United States Constitution would supersede, or have power over, other laws. The Constitution is the final law of the land, and all other laws must work in accord with it. Some or all of the uses of non-English listed by English Plus and MALDEF members, as well as those listed by U.S. English, could be illegal under a constitutional amendment, depending on how strongly the amendment was written. The importance of an ELA, therefore, cannot be underestimated.

ARIZONA OFFICIAL ENGLISH LAW CHALLENGED

In 1990, in the absence of a U.S. constitutional English Language Amendment, an employee in Arizona was able to use the U.S. Constitution to overrule her state's Official English amendment.

Maria-Kelly Yniguez was an Arizona state insurance claims manager. Before Arizona passed its English language amendment in 1988, Yniguez spoke

Spanish when necessary. She used her bilingual skills to help Spanish-speaking people who wanted to file medical malpractice insurance claims. She spoke English with English-speaking people.

After Arizona's English language amendment passed, Yniguez stopped speaking Spanish. She filed a lawsuit claiming that Arizona's law violated her First Amendment rights. The First Amendment of the U.S. Constitution guarantees freedom of speech. Her freedom of speech, she charged, was being taken away.

A federal judge agreed, ruling that Arizona's English language amendment was unconstitutional. Bilingual supporters had won. Official English supporters had lost. At least for the moment.

Attorney Kathryn Imahara, though pleased that the judge struck down Arizona's law, explains that this does not mean that all Official English laws and amendments are unconstitutional. Arizona's law was more restricting than most. Some of the state laws, such as California's, have no real force to them. California's amendment, until the state legislators pass a law that says how it will be enforced, has no more practical impact than saying that the California poppy is the state flower, explains Imahara. Arizona's amendment, however, included rules that all government business had to be conducted in English only. This meant that even state senators who had been elected by Spanish-speaking voters could not speak to them in Spanish. And all business at City Hall, including government information given out to Spanish-speaking citizens, had to be in English. U.S. District Court Judge Paul G. Rosenblatt explained that Arizona's amendment was unconstitutional because all of these regulations took away an American's right to freedom of speech.[16]

U.S. English vowed to fight the court's decision. S.I. Hayakawa, in *The New York Times*, said, "The decision is

71

creating a chilling effect in other states where official-English laws are being considered or implemented [put into effect]."[17]

But before the year was out, U.S. English had successfully pushed forward Alabama's constitutional amendment and was moving onto campaigns in other target states. Meanwhile, in Arizona, Arizonans for Official English were trying to get a new day in court to challenge Judge Rosenblatt's decision.

"YOU MAY" OR "YOU SHALL"

The traditional pattern of immigrants—coming to the United States, giving up their languages, and taking on English—is being broken by today's newcomers, say Official English advocates.

For the first time, said a U.S. English spokesperson, the United States has immigrants who do not believe it is their responsibility to learn English. "We have Koreans saying, 'We are Korean, and we are special. What's important to us is our language and our culture and we're going to retain that.' "[18]

English Plus leaders disagree. Mary Carol Combs, writing on behalf of English Plus, argues that first- and second-generation immigrants *are* shifting to English. She referred to a study of Hispanics in the United States, a group that comes under some of the heaviest attack in language battles. "Although only half of Mexican-American immigrants themselves have a working knowledge of English, more than 95 percent of first-generation Mexican-Americans born in the U.S. are proficient [skilled] in English; of the second generation, more than half speak only English," she said. This shows that today's immigrants are, indeed, learning English at least as fast as did immigrants before them.

English Plus leaders also point out that there is a great desire among immigrant groups to learn English.

*Tape recorders help these immigrants
study English in Washington, D.C.*

In California, in the same year that Californians voted for their English language amendment, says Combs, there were more than forty thousand people in Los Angeles on a waiting list for English instruction.[19]

Time, money, and effort should be spent on increasing English-learning opportunities, bilingual advocates point out, not on trying to pass laws to restrict other languages. Bilingual leaders agree that English is the language of opportunity in the United States. And it's important that all citizens have the opportunity to learn the language.

Bilingual advocates explain that they oppose the Official English laws and constitutional amendments not because they disagree with the importance of knowing English, but because they disagree with the message that Official English laws send. "It's different to say, 'Let's all learn English' than to say 'You *shall* learn English,'" explains Kathryn Imahara. The amendments say "You shall" and they close the doors to opportunity that bilingual ballots and bilingual job or government information signs and brochures open up. They tell minority-language Americans that their mother tongue is not as good as English. It insinuates that their culture is not as good. And it hints that they, as people, are not as good. There's a "kind of arrogance" to the Official English laws, says Imahara. And the message is that "you [minority language people] must rise to our [English-speaking] level."

Instead of passing these kinds of laws, she adds, "both sides need to try more to get to know their neighbors."[20] And to understand each other with sympathy, not hostility.

5
BILINGUAL EDUCATION PROGRAMS: HOW THEY WORK

Bilingual education is a political issue as much as it is an educational one—maybe even more so. Controversy swirls around almost all discussions of the subject. Politicians at all levels of government, from school boards to senatorial chambers, argue over the use of languages other than English in U.S. classrooms. They argue over whether or not bilingual programs should be approved at all by the government, and they argue over what *kinds* of bilingual programs should be allowed. They argue over the financing of programs. And they debate back and forth about what the goals of bilingual education should be.

Politicians, not educators, control the government's budget. Therefore politicians, not educators, control what kinds of programs schools will offer to children with limited English skills. And politicians are divided on the issue. In the same way that political leaders take sides on whether or not English should legally be made the official language of the United

States, they are divided over whether or not American classrooms should be conducted only in English.

Even the goal of bilingual education, which must be decided before any real agreement can be reached on the specific issues within bilingual education, has come into question of late. The *official* goal of bilingual education in the United States for the last several years has been to teach English to non-English-speaking students and to propel them into classrooms conducted solely in English; that is, to "mainstream" them. But is this the best and only goal a bilingual program can hope to achieve? Some Americans say no. They are wondering if students must give up their first languages in order to learn a second. Shouldn't bilingual-education programs encourage true bilingualism instead of expecting students to forfeit their first language and replace it with English? Or are the United States' schools responsible solely for the English language and other native languages are the responsibility of students themselves? Or if bilingualism is not the goal, but it is the *result* of some programs, is this bad? Or is it good?

There are no definite answers. Educators cannot tell America's political leaders which goals show the most promise for the future of America's children because educators are also divided on the issue.

Bilingual education is not just one program that can be easily evaluated. It is a variety of programs. Technically, every bilingual-education program in the United States, by definition, includes English plus another language. But when politicians and educators debate over bilingual education, they are debating about *all* programs used to teach Limited English Skilled students. (Educators usually refer to students as Limited English Proficient, LEP, meaning that they have limited English skills in more than just speaking, but also in writing, reading, and comprehension. In this book, they will be called Limited English Skilled.)

Some of the programs for Limited English Skilled students use English only, with no other languages used in the classroom.

Educators are divided over which programs work best. A certain program may work in one school, but not in another. Though the program is important, so are the ability of the teachers, the dedication of the students, and the support of the community. Countless factors, large and small, come together to make a program succeed or fail.

Consequently, it is not uncommon to have one educator supporting bilingual-education programs and another opposing them. One educator wants bilingual programs vastly increased; another wants them virtually eliminated. Every educator wants the same result. They want students to learn. They are divided only over what methods should be used to teach them.

For all of us, the first step to understanding the bilingual-education controversy is to sort out what bilingual education is and how some of the programs work.

A RAINBOW OF BILINGUAL PROGRAMS

If educators and politicians have agreed on anything in the bilingual-education controversy, it is that there are too many different combinations of students in American classrooms for one program to fit the needs of all. One class may have students speaking several different languages, including Vietnamese, Spanish, and Farsi; another may have half of its students speaking Chinese, the other half English; still another class might include just two or three Spanish-speaking children in a room full of native English speakers. What single program could possibly work equally well in all these different situations?

Of course, no single program can work in all situations. Therefore, educators have developed several distinctly different bilingual-education programs. And then they combine techniques from them in various ways to come up with their own custom programs. The editors of *Education Week* explain, however, that all of the programs can be classified into three basic types of approaches: Transitional Bilingual Education, Immersion, and English as a Second Language programs. Keep in mind that teachers often apply techniques of all three approaches in one classroom.

TRANSITIONAL BILINGUAL EDUCATION. Transitional, or temporary, bilingual programs use students' native languages to teach them their school subjects until they learn English well enough to attend all their classes in English. In a typical program, students might begin by attending art, music, and physical education classes in English. Their other subjects—reading, mathematics, science, and social studies—will be taught in their native language. As they gradually learn English, they will move into English mathematics classes, then the other classes, until they study all their subjects completely in English.

Maintenance bilingual education follows a similar pattern, except that a teacher strives to help students maintain, or keep, their first language while they are learning English. In this method, a teacher concentrates on helping students add a new language and new customs while at the same time helping them hold on to, and often learn more about, their own native language and customs.

In some maintenance bilingual programs in American schools, teachers include native English speakers in the classes alongside limited English speakers. In these programs, called two-way (or dual language) bilingual education, while Spanish-speaking students, for example, are learning English, English-speaking students are learning Spanish. Both groups of students sit in the same classroom, and study all their subjects side by side. The teacher instructs first in one language, then in the other, alternating back and forth. Educators who teach this way hope that students will learn to understand and respect each other's cultures. And they believe that a second language will one day be an asset to the native English-speaking students involved.

IMMERSION. These programs use English as the language of instruction. This is chiefly a monolingual (one-language) approach to teaching. Even though the students themselves might speak and understand little or no English, teachers instruct in English. They use a variety of techniques—body language, visual aids, simple sentence constructions—to get their point across to students, but they avoid using the students' native language.

Many versions of this kind of program are being used in today's schools. In most, teachers use the English-only approach. In some programs, teachers who are themselves bilingual may allow students to ask questions in their native language, but the teachers answer in English.

Immersion is not "submersion," the sink-or-swim approach. In submersion, students receive no special language help. Though they may enter a classroom knowing no English, they are expected to learn it on their own and to catch up to their fellow English-speaking classmates. They are, in a sense, tossed into the classroom pool and left to their own devices to either learn to "swim" the English language or to "sink" to the bottom of the educational pool.

The sink-or-swim submersion method has fallen far out of favor in the United States. Immersion, though it may often be confused with submersion, is not at all the same thing.

ENGLISH AS A SECOND LANGUAGE. Commonly called ESL, this is used widely in American schools. It is not

*Hawthorne Elementary School in San Francisco,
California, received an award of excellence in
1989 for its innovative bilingual education
program. Pictured here is a kindergarten class in action.*

really a program as much as it is a combination of methods used to teach English to non-English speakers. Educators have developed several classroom methods of teaching English, some with and some without the use of other languages to help in translation. When they use these methods to teach English in the classroom, they are teaching "English as a Second Language." For some schools, this is the only bilingual-education program offered. For others, it is just one part of a larger program.

Students in schools that have ESL classes but nothing else usually take these English classes in addition to their regular classes, which are taught in English. Often this means that the children will leave their classmates a few times each week for this separate instruction.[1]

Each one of these bilingual-education methods, and each combination of these methods employed by teachers in schools across the nation, has its champions—those who think it works best of all. And each one, too, has its critics—those who think, for one reason or another, that the program is unsuitable.

The following examples, including bilingual maintenance programs, a two-way Immersion program, and an ESL-based program, combine the several techniques of bilingual education. Interestingly, all of these programs are successes. Interestingly, too, they are all very different from each other.

A NAVAJO BILINGUAL SCHOOL

In Rock Point, Arizona, on the Navajo reservation, parents and teachers together created a bilingual-education program especially designed for their Navajo children. The program uses the Navajo language and English, so that students graduating from it are truly bilingual and biliterate, able to speak, read, and write in both English and Navajo.

The Rock Point program is "one of the best-known success stories in Indian bilingual education,"[2] according to *Education Week*. It tackles an often overlooked bilingual-education challenge, that of teaching Native American children. Many of these young Americans come to the first day of school speaking only their own tribal language. Others speak a limited version of English. They have picked up a cross section of languages, combining some English words, for example, with some tribal sentence structure, ending up with an "Indian English." Says Dick Littlebear, president of the Montana Association for Bilingual Education, "You find these kids floating between two nonstandard languages, a population growing up without a linguistic [language] home."[3]

The Rock Point Navajo bilingual program was developed over more than two decades. The local school board was made up of Navajo parents and adults. And they cooperated with the district's teachers to design their own custom program. The basis for the program, say Agnes and Wayne Holm, two of the educators responsible for developing it, is "a concern for quality education in two languages [and] for Navajo-ness." The teachers also wanted the program to have some meaning for the Navajo students. And they wanted parents and others in the community to be involved in running the program.

"The school was a talking school," say the Holms. "There was a very Navajo, very matter-of-fact feel about the school; students were on task [working] most of the time. . . . This low hum of meaningful student talk contrasted markedly with the sometimes deathly silence of some more seatwork-oriented Reservation schools, or the near chaos between classes in some other Reservation schools."

The program is straightforward. Kindergarten students come to school half-days, and they have three teachers, two Navajo-speaking teachers and one English-speaking teacher. They spend about two-thirds of their time in their new schoolroom learning in Navajo.

First- and second-graders have two teachers, and they spend about equally as much time learning in Navajo as they do in English. Some of their more difficult subjects are taught in the Navajo language. And before they read in English, they learn to read in Navajo. It's not until they are in the second grade, after they've learned to read in Navajo, that they are given English books to read. "We did not replace reading in Navajo," the Holms emphasize, "we added reading in English. Thereafter, students were expected to read and write in both languages."

The first- and second-graders are taught math in both Navajo and English, learning mathematic skills, such as adding or subtracting, first in their stronger language, Navajo, and then picking up English terms in their math-in-English classes.

In third through sixth grade, children have an English-language teacher and they learn in English about two-thirds of their time. For about one-third of each day, though, they leave their homeroom and study with a Navajo-language teacher who teaches Navajo literacy, Navajo social studies, and science-in-Navajo.

Once they get to junior high, students spend about 85 to 90 percent of their classroom time with English-speaking teachers, but they maintain their Navajo fluency and learn more about Navajo culture in science-in-Navajo courses and in Navajo language projects. And finally, when they are in high school, Navajo students spend about 90 to 95 percent of their time learning in English, but once again maintain their Navajo with Navajo courses taught in Navajo.

*Boys at a Navajo school show
their enthusiasm for reading.*

High-school students study Navajo history, Navajo social problems, Navajo government, and Navajo economic development. When they graduate, say the Holms, they are "among the few students on the Reservation who [leave] high school with some formal preparation for participation in the Navajo political process." And that kind of preparation cannot be scoffed at. The Navajos are proprietors of this country's largest single Native American reservation.

"The school tried to practice, not just to preach, that every student was expected to succeed," explain the Holms. "Most did; most came to expect that they and others could and would do so."[4]

EAST LOS ANGELES

In another bilingual-education project much like the Rock Point Navajo program, teachers use Spanish in classrooms dominated by Spanish-speaking children. The teachers report that they, too, have high expectations of their students, and they, too, have had successes. It operates in Los Angeles, California, and is one of the best-known programs in the country. In the Los Angeles Unified School District, there are more than 620,000 students. Of these, 213,306, or 35 percent, were Limited English Skilled in 1989–1990. Ninety percent of the Limited English Skilled students spoke Spanish. The rest of the students spoke Korean, Armenian, Cantonese, Vietnamese, Pilipino, Farsi, and other languages.[5]

The Los Angeles program began with an experimental program in East Los Angeles, a low-income area with a majority of Spanish-speaking people. It has since been used as a blueprint for several other programs in California and other states.

In this program, students learn language skills first in Spanish. But they do not learn just to read in Spanish. They also develop thinking, reasoning, and creative skills in Spanish. In addition to learning Spanish and to being taught some of their subjects in Spanish, the young students also take English as a Second Language classes and learn some subjects in English. But until about the fourth grade, or sometimes the fifth, the children study in Spanish.

"One of the things that's exciting [about this program] is, you can walk into a classroom and the second graders are doing science experiments and talking, talking—they're doing committee work. These are the same kids that in another [program] would be just sitting there wondering what was going on, or in a corner with a translator,"[6] says Bonnie Rubio, one of the Los Angeles educators who started the program.

The program is based on a theory similar to that of the Rock Point Navajo program: If children learn language skills completely in one language—any language—then those skills will transfer to another language—that is, English.

What's also important about the program and others like it is that it helps Limited English Skilled young students keep up with the thinking skills other students their ages are learning. Los Angeles education official Maria Ott explains that in kindergarten through grade two, especially, children build the foundations for thinking. In these early grades, teachers are helping students develop organized thinking patterns, and creative skills that they will later build on to do complicated mathematics and critical thinking. In order for these skills to develop, however, students must completely understand the language they are being taught in. Ott adds that though children with limited English often understand the simple things their classmates say to them on the playground, they often do not understand the more complicated things teachers say to them. That's why, she says, her program uses Spanish in the early grades—so Spanish-speaking students can learn these important thinking skills as well as the English-speaking students learn them.[7] A by-product of the program, adds Bonnie Rubio, is that students end up being bilingual.[8]

NEW YORK IMMERSION PROGRAM

In a program in New York City, which also heavily uses the Spanish language, officials claim success. They also claim that "language itself is not taught; rather, it is learned through use in informal classroom structures." The program is a dual-language program, explains Sidney H. Morison, who was the principal of Public School 84 when the program was started. It's an "enrichment" program, he says. And it works two ways. At P.S. 84, English-speaking children learn Spanish, while Spanish-speaking children learn English.

About 53 percent of the school's elementary students were Hispanic in the 1990 school year. In the school, Spanish is spoken socially and officially. Above the school entrance, student-made signs say WELCOME and BIENVENIDO. Inside, along with English signs, are signs in Spanish—SALIDA, OFICINA, SALÓN DE MÉDICO. Parents receive school letters and notes in both languages. A bilingual secretary speaks Spanish or English, as the situation demands, talking to one person on the phone in Spanish, to one of the children in English, to a parent in English, to a child in Spanish, back and forth. And in the halls, children and teachers are as likely to be speaking Spanish as they are English.

But P.S. 84's program is not a traditional bilingual program, Morison explains. Though it has some likeness to a two-way bilingual-education program, teachers in P.S. 84's program use the Immersion approach. They do not translate for the children.

Children in kindergarten, first, and second grade learn in English one day and in Spanish the next. They do not repeat lessons from day to day. The students

87

need to understand Monday's math lesson in Spanish in order to understand Tuesday's math lesson in English. On an English day, teachers do not speak Spanish; on a Spanish day, they do not use English.

In third and fourth grade, the students alternate teachers as well as languages, learning from a Spanish-speaking teacher one day, and English-speaking teacher the next. In fifth and sixth grade, students learn social studies and some math from Spanish-language teachers, which accounts for about 35 percent of their time, but study the rest of the time in English.

"The primary aim of the dual-language program," says Morison, "is academic growth." Teachers hope that all their students will graduate from sixth grade with a solid education in all subjects. A by-product of the program is that students become bilingual and biliterate in Spanish and English. Spanish-language children do not lose their Spanish; they add English. English-language children add Spanish. All students are taught to respect and appreciate the languages and customs of each other.

Morison found a further benefit of his school's immersion program, too. "In the immersion context," he says, "children also seem to be more attentive than we remember them being before the dual language program began."[9] They search for clues when listening in their weaker language. They watch the teacher closely, and they watch the reactions of other children. In the school's earlier program, where teachers often translated back and forth for the children, the children tuned out the less familiar language and simply waited for explanations in their first language.

ESL PROGRAM IN MASSACHUSETTS

In yet another program, educators base their classes on English as a Second Language structure. Their students are taught English as quickly as possible, and no attempt is made to maintain their first language. Yet this program, different as it is from the Navajo, Los Angeles, and New York programs, is equally as successful. The program is being used in Newton, Massachusetts, schools. It serves a group of students who speak a variety of different languages and come from an array of nations.

Thirty-one different languages were spoken by the 348 limited-English students in the district in 1989. Some of the students spoke Cantonese, others Farsi, French, Spanish, Vietnamese, Korean, Khmer, Mandarin, Japanese, Hebrew, Greek, Italian; one spoke Bengali, and still another spoke Foochow.

The children's backgrounds varied widely, too. Some had very good academic training and others had little or no schooling. Thirty percent of the children were refugees from Southeast Asia, Iran, Afghanistan, Russia, and Central America. Forty percent were immigrants from Italian and Asian families. And the rest were children of visiting scholars and professionals from Japan, Israel, Europe, and South America.

The plan used to teach all these children, says Rosalie Pedalino Porter, ESL and bilingual program director for the Newton, Massachusetts, public schools, includes elements of Immersion, ESL, and bilingual methods. English as a Second Language classes, however, form the program's foundation.

Students entering the Newton district schools are tested in English and math, and the results of those tests determine how many hours of ESL classes the students will attend.

In the ESL classrooms, teachers use an Immersion technique. They use films, videos, songs, drama, and real objects to get their message across without needing to speak the students' native languages. "English, in simplified form at first but gradually more sophisticated," explains Porter, is used to introduce students to mathematics, science, and social studies, so that even though the new students are spending their time in an English class, they are also learning some of the things their schoolmates are learning in their mainstream classes taught in English.

New students spend from one to three hours a day in their ESL classes, reducing those hours as they get better in English. The rest of their day they spend in mainstream classrooms, with English-speaking teachers, at first in just art, music, and physical education classes. Their mainstream class hours are increased as they learn English, with mathematics, science, social studies, and other subjects being added as the students are ready.

The Newton school district also has a few bilingual teachers and teacher's aides who can teach in Spanish, Japanese, Hebrew, or Chinese. When the district has several children in one grade all speaking one of these languages, then these teachers hold bilingual classes. But even here, says Porter, the emphasis is on learning *in* English. "[Teachers] use English for instruction from the first day," says Porter, "and the use of the native language is decreased rapidly during the first year, serving mainly to promote a comfortable school adjustment."

Since witnessing the success of her district's ESL program, Porter now challenges bilingual-education methods that allow children to study in their native language. Newton's program produces English-speaking students who score on their tests at the same grade level as their native English-speaking classmates; they seldom skip school; they generally have a positive self-image and are "well integrated with their classmates, and participate in many [school] activities,"[10] says Porter.

Newton's program, Porter concludes, meets all the requirements and desires of America's educational system. It provides equal educational opportunity to limited-English students, and it teaches students the English language.

There's no real agreement within the educational community over which program works best—ESL, Immersion, bilingual teaching methods, or any combination of these. Every school is unique, with its own set of problems and its own individual blend of students. Educators across the country study the programs that have been successful. They then try to adapt these to their own students' needs. And while educators seek the program that works best for their students, the nation's political leaders argue over the different methods. Politicians seek political solutions to the bilingual-education problem. They line up in support of, or against, the different programs. And in Washington, D.C., senators and representatives try to set up a national policy for bilingual education.

6
THE POLITICS OF BILINGUAL EDUCATION

A Mexican-American girl who grew up to be a member of the board of the Los Angeles Unified School District recalls what it was like for her when she moved to America. She was thirteen, and in her old school in Juárez, Mexico, she had been a straight-A student. In her new school in California, she was getting Fs.

It wasn't that the subjects were more difficult—they weren't. The problem was that she couldn't understand what the teacher was saying. The teacher only spoke English. Leticia spoke only Spanish. "I experienced a lot of . . . anger and embarrassment," Leticia Quezada says now. She learned English as quickly as possible, studying the new, strange words for hours every night after school. She even slept with a dictionary under her pillow.

She is one of the success stories of American immigrants. She graduated from college and earned a master's degree in education. But she knows she is an exception.[1]

Quezada came to the United States in the 1960s.

Though she may not have felt it at the time, the United States was going through an awakening. In 1964, the Civil Rights Act was passed. A critically important stepping-stone to equality for African-Americans and other American minorities, the act bans discrimination based on race, color, religion, national origin, or sex.

The Civil Rights Act was passed with the support of President Lyndon Baines Johnson. And it came at a time when Martin Luther King, Jr., was leading the nation toward more respectful relations among its many minority groups and the majority. Also at that time, encouraged by the advances among African-Americans, Hispanics in the Southwest were demanding change. One of the improvements they wanted was bilingual education for the large numbers of Hispanic children who were failing in English-only schools.[2]

Changes were already in the wind. In September 1963, in Florida, an experimental bilingual program sponsored by the Ford Foundation was begun. The program mixed English-speaking children with Cuban Spanish-speaking children in a two-way system at Coral Way Elementary School in Dade County. Most of the Cuban children in the program were the sons and daughters of refugees from the 1959 Cuban Revolution. The Coral Way program the children took part in, explains one bilingualism expert, was "the first resurrection of bilingual education in the United States in recent history."[3] In fact, says another expert, it was "the nation's first in probably half a century."[4] And the program was a success. Within a decade, Dade County officials had expanded it to include 3,683 elementary students (2,608 of them Spanish-speaking) and to include about 2,000 secondary-school children as well.[5]

The great wave of Cuban immigrants into Dade County and their bilingual needs helped to trigger a national discussion of bilingual education. The demands of Hispanic students in the Southwest added to the issue, and bilingual education found a spotlight in political debate.

The political climate for change was good. Lyndon Johnson was still president. And although tremendous demonstrations and conflicts over civil rights and the Vietnam War rocked the United States, the country was confident that positive changes could be made.

The nation was willing to spend money on new, and sometimes experimental, bilingual programs. In 1967, Texas Senator Ralph Yarborough and six cosponsors introduced the American Bilingual Education Act on the Senate floor. Originally, Senator Yarborough intended his bilingual-education bill just for Spanish-speaking children in American schools. The senator told his colleagues that Anglos in the southwestern states were averaging 12 years of school for those who were fourteen years of age and over. But Spanish-surnamed children, he said, averaged just 8.1 years. And, he added, "my own state of Texas ranks at the bottom." There, Spanish-surnamed children averaged only 4.7 years of school.[6] Yarborough and other bilingual-education supporters hoped that bilingual programs would encourage children to stay in school and graduate.

The concept of bilingual education, says James J. Lyons, a Washington attorney, "proved politically popular, and soon more than three dozen bilingual-education bills were introduced in the House of Representatives."[7]

Senators and representatives debated the bilingual-education act. They considered information on the psychology of students, on what makes them succeed or drop out, and on experimental bilingual programs in existence at the time. The Coral Way Elementary School program was brought up and studied again and again. It was an important example of how bilingual education could work. It provided "a powerful fact," says Walter G. Secada of the University of Wisconsin. Research at Coral Way documented the difficulties Spanish-speaking children faced in English classrooms. And the program provided an example of what could be done to remove those difficulties.[8] It was also used to overrule arguments from politicians who opposed bilingual education.

The act that was finally signed by President Johnson in 1968 made funds available to all minority-language programs. The BEA, as the Bilingual Education Act came to be known, was officially an amendment to the Elementary and Secondary Education Act of 1965. It set up a federal system to provide money for bilingual-education programs for limited-English-speaking children from low-income families. (In the 1974 amendment to the BEA, the low-income requirement was dropped.)

The BEA was important, as it gave bilingual programs a place in the federal budget. But it did not *require* schools to establish bilingual programs. The funds were simply there if schools wanted to apply for them.

The BEA left at least one thing unclear: What kinds of bilingual programs would the federal government prefer? And which programs would be first in line for funding? Legislators turned their attention to these questions and the debate over bilingual education continued.

SCHOOL SALADS AND MELTING POTS

The Coral Way program was a "pluralist" program. It encouraged bilingualism in Spanish-speaking children, as well as in English-speaking children. It could also be called a maintenance program, as it maintained, or held onto, a student's native-language abilities while adding English to his or her skills. In this respect, this program encouraged students to maintain

Bilingual kindergarten students in San Francisco begin to learn to read. The poster at the far right is in Spanish.

their cultural attachments and become ingredients in an American salad.

Other programs, such as Transitional Bilingual Education and Immersion, are not concerned with maintaining students' first languages. They are instead concerned solely with teaching English, and are usually seen as assimilation programs. They encourage students to become "Americanized," and part of the melting pot. But, chiefly, they leave the job of holding onto native languages and heritages to the students and their families. Some of the best of all of these kinds of programs have worked with excellent results, as seen in the chapter 5 descriptions of the New York City Public School 84 maintenance program and the Newton, Massachusetts, transitional program.

Regardless of how well the programs work, however, the decision of which programs receive funds and, therefore, which of them are used, has been, and continues to be, a political decision. And fundamental to the debate over this decision is whether a program encourages a plural, "salad," society or an assimilated, "melting-pot," society.

BILINGUAL EDUCATION—NEW RULES

The Bilingual Education Act went into effect in a political climate that was somewhat open-minded on this issue. The country's attention was focused on busing, integration of schools, and civil rights. Americans were concerned about minorities, and many, minority and majority alike, seemed eager to end discrimination and prejudice in the nation. Richard M. Nixon moved into the White House in 1969. Over the next few years the Nixon administration urged schools to reduce discrimination toward minority-language students, and also urged schools toward greater fairness to African-Americans.

Nixon's Department of Health, Education, and

97

Welfare sent out guidelines to school districts in 1970 reminding them of the law—telling them that they were responsible for educating *all* students equally. Nixon's administration seemed bent on ending discrimination and on providing equal opportunity for every student. His department gave school officials some specific rules to follow. A few of those rules: Schools were to make college preparatory courses available to all students, regardless of English skills; they were to move limited-English speakers into mainstream classes and to stop segregating them in dead-end tracks; when necessary for understanding, school administrators were to send some notices to minority-language parents in the parents' language.[9] Nixon's administration seemed to be supporting most of the goals of the new Bilingual Education Act.

At the same time as Nixon's administration was developing its rules and its plans for funding bilingual-education programs, a group of Chinese students in San Francisco's public schools were becoming more and more unhappy with the quality of the education they were receiving. The students numbered nearly 3,000 in a school district of 16,500 pupils. The parents of the Chinese students took the school system to court—all the way to the Supreme Court of the United States—because most of the students were receiving no bilingual help in their classrooms.

The case was called *Lau v. Nichols,* and the Supreme Court heard it in 1974. The Chinese parents told the court that about two-thirds of their children were in all-English classes. The Bilingual Education Act did not require schools to have bilingual classes. The parents argued, however, that their children were not receiving a fair and equal education because the youngsters couldn't understand what the teachers were saying. Therefore they were not learning as much as the English-speaking students in the area's schools.

The Supreme Court decided the parents were right. Justice William O. Douglas, who wrote the Court's opinion, said, "There is no equality of treatment merely by providing students with the same facilities, textbooks, teachers, and curriculum; for students who do not understand English are effectively foreclosed from any meaningful education."[10] If the students couldn't understand what the teachers were saying, then they weren't getting an equal education. The school district, the Court added, was also breaking the rules that Nixon's administration had sent to them. Finally, though the Court did *not* tell the schools how to run a program that would be fair to limited-English students, it did order the board of education to correct the situation.[11]

Lau v. Nichols is the most important court case in bilingual-education's recent history. It set the stage for expanded bilingual programs and even today is the basis for many arguments in favor of bilingual education. The fact that it did not specify what kinds of bilingual programs are acceptable left this aspect open to continued debate.

The year the case was decided, 1974, was the same year Nixon resigned from office. Gerald Ford became president, supporting bilingual-education goals, and directing his administration to become aggressive and make sure that schools were being fair to their limited-English students.

Ford's Department of Health, Education, and Welfare wrote up new guidelines. These came to be known as the *Lau Remedies.*

These new guidelines outlined specific methods that school officials were to use in their federally funded programs for limited-English-speaking children. The remedies told teachers how to judge the children's English skills, how to choose which programs these children needed, how to decide which students were ready to move out of special-language classes and into mainstream classes, and how to decide what skills were needed by the teachers of these classes.

The *Lau Remedies* also told school officials that English as a Second Language programs, if these were the only ones offered in elementary schools, were not enough. Schools had to do more. The remedies required schools to use bilingual-education methods: Schools had to use students' native languages in the classrooms. They might use the language in a transitional program that provided second-language help only until students could learn in English. Or schools might use a bilingual-bicultural method that developed fluency in both English and a second language. Or schools might even have a multilingual, multicultural method that developed fluency in at least three languages. But in one way or another, they must use the native language.

The *Lau Remedies* were quite specific in what schools could do and how they could do it. This specific nature of the remedies was to come under attack later. But for a time, while first President Ford and then President Jimmy Carter led the nation, the *Lau Remedies* were strongly supported and enforced. Between 1975 and 1980, the federal government examined nearly 600 programs to see if they were following the guidelines set up by the *Lau Remedies.* As a result of these reviews, 359 school-district plans for bilingual education programs were corrected, begun, or changed in some way.[12] Carter's administration was on the side of bilingual education, and was enforcing the law in favor of bilingual programs.

President Carter encouraged his Democratic administration to use its clout to make bilingual programs available to all schools that wanted them. Carter tried to make bilingual education work. He believed that it could offer Limited English Skilled students a fair chance at a good education.

As he came toward the end of his one term in office, though, Carter found himself fighting a tough political battle with conservatives in Congress over the federal role in education.

As bilingual education had grown, through Johnson's, Nixon's, Ford's, and Carter's terms in office, the federal government had assumed more and more of a supervising role in bilingual programs. Conservatives complained that education, which had once been a purely local or statewide responsibility, was coming more and more under the direction of the federal government. Liberals, on the other hand, supported the switch, arguing that federal control was necessary to promote fairness across the land.

Meanwhile, President Carter was in the final stages of running for reelection. He had appointed Shirley M. Hufstedler, a federal judge on the Ninth Circuit Court of Appeals, to head his new Department of Education. On August 5, 1980, she issued new rules for bilingual programs seeking federal monies. Her new rules were even more specific than the previous *Lau Remedies* had been. Carter's political opponents reacted angrily and quickly to the new rules. Hufstedler received more than four thousand letters, "most of them critical."[13] And Hufstedler's new bilingual-education rules became part of the political debate between Carter and the conservative Republican candidate for office, Ronald Reagan.

Hufstedler agreed to stop action on the new rules, but the political damage had been done. The educational problem was just one small factor that affected the 1980 presidential elections. Many major events were hotly debated at the time. Carter lost to Ronald Reagan in a resounding defeat.

Times were changing. The political wrangling during the presidential campaign weakened support for bilingual education. Ronald Reagan brought a conservative outlook to the White House. In off-the-cuff remarks shortly after taking office, President Reagan assured Americans that he thought bilingual education was necessary. But he indicated that he believed it should be more limited than it was.

"I think it is proper that we have teachers equipped who can get at them in their own language and understand why it is they don't get the answer to the problem and help them in that way,"[14] said Reagan. "But," he added when talking to a group of mayors, "it is absolutely wrong and against American concept to have a bilingual education program that is now openly, admittedly dedicated to preserving their native language and never getting them adequate in English so they can go out into the job market."[15]

President Reagan's new secretary of education, Terrel H. Bell, withdrew the rules that Carter's Secretary Hufstedler had written. The *Lau Remedies*, which had been the government's way of ensuring that schools developed bilingual programs, were no longer enforced. Without enforcement of the *Lau Remedies* that had specifically told school officials to use a second language in classrooms, schools were free to develop their own programs for Limited English Skilled students. Reagan's administration, in fact, encouraged schools to develop their own individual programs.

President Reagan's conservative administration was putting a stop to the expansion of bilingual-education programs that used native languages in the classroom, rerouting education for limited-English students onto a different road. In 1983, President Reagan "mobilized to slash the federal budget for bilingual education,"[16] says one bilingual expert. And during his eight years in office, between 1980 and 1988, spending for Bilingual Education Act programs was cut by 47 percent.

Meanwhile, the debate over bilingual education became, even more than ever before, a debate over what kinds of programs should be used for students with limited English skills.

The Reagan administration focused its energies on trying to get rid of one of the Bilingual Education Act's requirements: that programs must use students' native languages in the teaching process.

A shift from a salad to a melting-pot approach was getting under way. The salad approach, which supported fluency in more than one language—true bilingualism—was being challenged by those supporting an English-only, traditional melting-pot theory.

In 1984, when the Bilingual Education Act came up for renewal, Congress debated the many kinds of bilingual education. It was a presidential election year, and President Reagan did not get directly involved in the debate, but Congress knew his administration's goals were to cut out the native-language requirement and to spend more on English-Only Immersion programs and English as a Second Language programs and less on transitional or maintenance bilingual programs.

Senators listened to arguments from the National Association for Bilingual Education (NABE), whose members argued that bilingual programs had made a difference in the academic success and self-esteem of many students. The NABE also argued that well-educated bilingual students were a resource that could benefit the country.

Legislators then listened to a counterargument presented to representatives in the House by U.S. English. This organization argued that the use of native languages in classrooms should be reduced and the government should support alternative educational methods—basically English-Only programs of Immersion, or limited use of English as a Second Language classes. They argued that programs using students' native languages had not proven that they could do the job, that is, teach English.[17]

After listening to both sides, legislators sided with supporters of programs using students' native languages, but they came up with a compromise. To please the more liberal congressional supporters of bilingual education, they granted 75 percent of the budget to programs that use students' native languages. Congress could also spend much of the rest of the money on Developmental Bilingual Programs, whose goals are bilingual fluency.

To please the more conservative congressional members, legislators created a special category of educational programs that they called Special Alternative Instruction Programs. These would be mostly English-Only or Immersion programs, and they would get 4 percent of the annual budget for bilingual education.

The legislators also decided it was time to write out new, clear goals for bilingual education. One goal of all bilingual programs, they said, was to teach English. But another goal was to help Limited English Skilled students meet graduation standards. The question of how to meet both of these goals remained a controversial one.

BUDGET SKIRMISHES

The Reagan administration continued, after the passage of the 1984 Bilingual Education Act, to push for more English Immersion programs and fewer programs using native languages. When Secretary Bell resigned, Reagan replaced him in 1985 with William J. Bennett, a strong supporter of English-Only Immersion programs.

Bennett kept the debate over bilingual education

going. Arguing that English-Only Immersion programs worked just as well as native-language programs, he tried to get Congress to give more than 4 percent of its budget to Immersion programs. In fact, he wanted Congress to remove the 4 percent limit entirely. Then more English-only programs could be funded, and fewer programs using native languages.

Supporters of programs using native languages argued that English-Only programs did not work as well as native-language ones. They held up a 1987 report from the federal government's own General Accounting Office: Most experts surveyed believed that students' native language should be used to some extent in the classroom. Most also said that there was not enough evidence to know if English-Only approaches worked.

Legislators were divided over the issue. In 1986, Senator Dan Quayle (R-IN), who two years later would be elected vice president, wrote an amendment to the Bilingual Education Act. He wanted what Secretary Bennett did, an increase in the amount of money spent on English-Only programs. His was one bill in a flurry of bilingual bills presented during that year, none of which were passed.[18]

Legislators received continuing pressure from conservatives and Reagan's Department of Education. Finally, in 1988, they passed an amendment to the Bilingual Education Act. They didn't lift the limit entirely, but they did change it to 25 percent. Bilingual-education programs that used students' native languages would continue to get 75 percent of the BEA budget; English-Only programs would get 25 percent; other programs could be paid for out of either side.

The fundamental question of whether American educators want to use two languages in the classroom or use English Only has not been answered. Further, the politics of Official English laws and constitutional amendments spills over into the politics and theories of education. Behind the arguments over bilingual education is the same question that lurks in all Official English debates: Is America a salad or a melting pot? Political leaders and educators alike strive to find a resolution to the arguments over these fundamental differences.

7
LOOKING FOR ANSWERS

In a perfect world, all people would cooperate and work toward a common goal of peace, productivity, and harmony. All languages would share equally in respect and status. So would all people. But this is not a perfect world. Clear thinking does not always rule. Emotions and desires also drive human beings. These emotions and desires are many and varied, and often they drive humans into conflict with each other. Wars rage. Battles are won and lost.

In today's debates over the English language, the battles being fought are political ones. They are just some of many political battles raging nationwide, even worldwide. But they are battles that are waged emotionally. There is more at stake here than simply whether one says *buenos días* or *hello*.

Underlying the battles are fears on one side that the center is not holding in America; that the society is being shattered into fragments; that people cannot communicate with one another and that they do not want to; that America will become a nation of mini-nations, of little Spanish cities, little Chinese cities, and little Cambodian cities, where English-speaking Americans are forced to either learn the region's language or leave.

Underlying the battles on the other side are fears that the English language is being used as a lock on a door to success. If other languages are outlawed and jobs, voting ballots, and opportunities are made available only to those who speak English, second-language Americans see themselves being locked out. They see their children going to school and being embarrassed, even feeling inferior, about their native language and culture.

Emotions run high. And they have run high at many times throughout American history, as language has again and again cropped up as a topic of debate. Anti-German feeling has been high during certain decades. Anti-Italian, -Polish, -Hungarian, -Japanese, -Chinese, -Pilipino, and many other antilanguage debates have raged. Possibly because the English language was not born in the United States, but was "adopted," explains why it has so often been called into question.

We ask ourselves, as the founders of the United States of America asked themselves, what makes a person an American? As people from around the world arrive at U.S. airports and borders, what do they share that makes them all potential Americans? Is the color of their skin important? Or the shape of their eyes? Or the sounds of their words? Today's immigrants are noticeably different from immigrants one hundred, or even fifty, years ago. Most of today's immigrants are Hispanic or Asian. But they come to the United States for many of the same reasons that previous generations of Americans came here. They come because they're hungry, as the Irish were during the potato famine of the mid-1800s. They come, rich and poor, because wars

108

at home threaten their lives, as Jewish Europeans came during World War II. They come because Communism or a dictatorship is taking over their countries, as Central Americans, Middle Easterners, and many others have come in this century.

When they arrive here, they follow some of the same patterns that previous generations of immigrants followed. They seek out others who have come here from the same country and speak the same language as they do. Cambodians find their way to Cambodian neighborhoods. Mexicans seek the comfort of other Mexicans. The newcomers also meet with some of the same difficulties that earlier immigrants did. They must find jobs for their wage earners, houses for their families, schools for their children. And they must learn English.

The debate over the English language is not really about whether or not Americans should all know English. It is about how best to present every American with the opportunity to learn English. Official English advocates say that laws are necessary to make sure that all newcomers to the United States, as well as all residents born here, learn English.

On the other side, many minority-language groups have united to argue that laws do not teach English, opportunity does. When job and social opportunities are open to minorities, then those minority people learn English so they can take advantage of those opportunities. When the Germans found the doors to business and social success open, they learned English so they could walk through those doors. When Hispanics and Asian-Americans see prejudice or discrimination closing the doors to the greater business community and to higher social circles, they have less incentive to learn English. They, turning back to their friends and neighbors, build a life for themselves separate from the greater community. The Official English

*As immigrants have so often done, people living in
this Chinese section sought out the company and
comfort of others like themselves. Now the neighborhood
reflects the Chinese heritage of these Americans.*

laws, they say, do not help people assimilate. They do not help people learn English.

"English-as-the-official-language resolutions," said California leaders opposed to the state's English language amendment in 1986, "will not help anyone learn English. They will not improve human relations, and they will not lead to a better community. They will create greater intergroup tension and ill will, encourage resentment and bigotry, pit neighbor against neighbor and group against group. They reflect our worst fears, not our best values."[1]

Official English advocates assure everyone that they are not seeking to increase bigotry in the United States. Indeed, they seek to reduce it by increasing communication among all Americans. The minority-language Americans who are against the Official English campaign respond that passing English-language laws only further isolates people.

Yet both sides believe that language is important to culture. It is central to the way citizens feel about their country, the way they express their loves and hates. Both sides, too, say that it is valuable in today's world for all Americans to speak two languages, and that all Americans need to speak English in order to succeed in this country.

The question about methods of achieving the goal of equal opportunity and communication for all Americans is the one that is truly in the hands of today's political leaders. It must be answered by America's legislators and leaders. And today's children and students must ask themselves these same questions about America: What path will take Americans to their goal of equal opportunity and harmony? And how will the guests speak at the celebration dinner when that goal is achieved? Will they speak English only? Or will they add their many languages to the dinner conversation?

111

Source Notes

CHAPTER ONE: PIONEERS OF MANY TONGUES
1. Robert McCrum, William Cran, and Robert MacNeil, *The Story of English* (New York: Elisabeth Sifton Books, Viking Penguin, 1986), 19.
2. Ibid.
3. Mark S. Hoffman, ed., *The World Almanac and Book of Facts, 1990* (New York: Pharos Books, 1990), 539.
4. McCrum, Cran, and MacNeil, *Story of English,* 19.
5. Stewart L. Udall, *To the Inland Empire: Coronado and Our Spanish Legacy* (Garden City, N.Y.: Doubleday, 1987), 24.
6. Ibid.
7. James Crawford, "Bilingual Education: Language, Learning, and Politics," *Education Week,* April 1, 1987, 21.
8. David Beers Quinn, *The Lost Colonists: Their Fortune and Probable Fate* (Raleigh, N.C.: North Carolina Division of Archives and History, 1984), 4.
9. David Freeman Hawke, *Everyday Life in Early America* (New York: Harper & Row, 1988), 100.
10. Bernard A. Weisberger, *The American People* (New York: American Heritage, 1970, 1971), 33.

11. McCrum, Cran, and MacNeil, *Story of English,* 239.
12. Stephen T. Wagner, "The Historical Background of Bilingualism and Biculturalism in the United States," in *The New Bilingualism: An American Dilemma* ed. Martin Ridge (New Brunswick, N.J.: Transaction Books— Rutgers University, 1981), 30.
13. "English Only: The Threat of Language Restrictions," *NALEO Background Paper Number 10,* 1989.
14. Wagner, "Historical Background," 30.
15. Weisberger, *American People,* 126.
16. Albert H. Marckwardt, revision by J. L. Dillard, *American English* (New York: Oxford University Press, 1958, 1980), 60–61.
17. Wagner, "Historical Background," 34.
18. Crawford, "Bilingual Education: Language, Learning, and Politics," p. 21.
19. McCrum, Cran, and MacNeil, *Story of English,* 123.
20. Marckwardt, *American English,* 48–49.
21. McCrum, Cran, and MacNeil, *Story of English,* 123–24.
22. Wagner, "Historical Background, 37, quoted from Theodore Roosevelt, "Americans Past and Present and the Americanization of Foreigners," *America,* April 14, 1888, 2.
23. Ibid., 42–43.
24. Ibid., 42, quoted from speech by Theodore Roosevelt, "America for Americans," St. Louis, Missouri, May 31, 1916, 3–4 (Cambridge, Mass.: Theodore Roosevelt Collection, Widener Library, Harvard University).
25. Crawford, "Bilingual Education," 22.

CHAPTER TWO: BILINGUAL COUNTRIES
OF THE WORLD
1. Kenji Hakuta, *Mirror of Language: The Debate on Bilingualism* (New York: Basic Books, 1986), 177.
2. Mark S. Hoffman, ed., *The World Almanac and Book of Facts 1990* (New York: Pharos Books, 1990), 743.
3. David Einhorn and Stela Ortiz Einhorn, "A Choice of Words," *Americas* 41, no. 1 (January/February 1989): 42.
4. Ibid.
5. Ibid., 47.

6. William L. Leap, "American Indian Languages," in *Language in the USA*, Charles A. Ferguson and Shirley Brice Heath (New York: Cambridge University Press, 1981), 116.
7. Ibid., 140.
8. Salomón Nahmad Sittón, "The Bilingual Experience in Mexico," in *The New Bilingualism: An American Dilemma*, ed. Martin Ridge (New Brunswick, N.J.: Transaction Books—Rutgers University, 1981), 94.
9. Ibid.
10. Ibid.
11. Ibid.
12. Martin Ridge, ed., *The New Bilingualism: An American Dilemma* (New Brunswick, N.J.: Transaction Books—Rutgers University, 1981), 126.
13. Greg W. Taylor, "Uncertain Survival," *Maclean's* 102, no. 45 (November 6, 1989): 30.
14. Maxwell F. Yalden, "The Bilingual Experience in Canada," in *The New Bilingualism: An American Dilemma*, ed. Martin Ridge (New Brunswick, N.J.: Transaction Books—Rutgers University, 1981), 74.
15. Ibid., 75.
16. Robert Fulford, "Canada, A Great Northern Paradox?" *Americas* 42, no. 1 (January/February 1990): 9.
17. Yalden, "Bilingual Experience in Canada," 75.
18. *The Canadian Encyclopedia*, vol. 2 (Edmonton, Canada: Hurtig Publishers, 1985), 976.
19. "The Return to Two Solitudes," *Maclean's* 102, no. 45 (November 6, 1989): 26.
20. Mary Williams Walsh, "A Tongue Lashing in Canada," *Los Angeles Times*, February 13, 1990, A1.
21. Christina Bratt Paulston, "Understanding Educational Policies in Multilingual States," *The Annals of the American Academy of Political and Social Science* 508 (March 1990): 45.
22. Robert McCrum, William Cram, and Robert MacNeil, *The Story of English* (New York: Elisabeth Sifton Books, Viking Penguin, 1986), 56.
23. Hoffman, *World Almanac*, 764.

24. Paulston, "Understanding Educational Policies," 42.
25. Carol J. Williams, "In Hungary, Learning Russian Is Out of Style," *Los Angeles Times,* June 15, 1990, A5.
26. John Paxton, ed., *The Statesman's Year-Book,* 125th ed. (New York: St. Martin's Press, 1988), 269.

CHAPTER THREE: WHY ARGUE OVER LANGUAGE?
 1. J. Sebastian Sinisi, "Official-English Backer Speaks at CU," *The Denver Post,* May 12, 1990, 1.
 2. U.S. Bureau of the Census, *U.S.A. Statistics in Brief 1990: A Statistical Abstract Supplement,* Washington, D.C., 1990.
 3. Thomas Morgan, "The Latinization of America," *Esquire,* May 1983, 47.
 4. Rick Holguin and George Ramos, "Cultures Follow Separate Paths in Huntington Park," *Los Angeles Times,* April 7, 1990, A30.
 5. Ibid., A31.
 6. S.I. Hayakawa, U.S. English press kit, including letter of solicitation, brochures, and flyers, received June 1990.
 7. Howard Banks, "Do We Want Quebec Here?" *Forbes,* June 11, 1990, 64.
 8. "The Balkans, U.S.A.," *National Review* 42, no. 4 (March 5, 1990): 19.
 9. Paul Cejas, Rosa Castro Feinberg, and S. I. Hayakawa, "The English-Only Debate," *Vista,* February 8, 1987, 13.
10. James C. Stalker, "Official English or English Only," *English Journal,* March 1988, 19.
11. William A. Henry III, "Beyond the Melting Pot," *Time,* April 9, 1990, 28.
12. Cejas, Feinberg, and Hayakawa, "English-Only Debate," 13.
13. Ibid.
14. Hayakawa, press kit.
15. Peter Brimelow, "A Cautionary Case of Bilingualism," *Commentary* 84, no. 5 (November 1987): 63.
16. Cejas, Feinberg, and Hayakawa, "English-Only Debate," 13.
17. Hayakawa, letter soliciting funds for U.S. English.
18. Brimelow, "Cautionary Case of Bilingualism," 63.

19. Cejas, Feinberg, and Hayakawa, 13.
20. Shirley Brice Heath, "English in Our Language Heritage," in *Language in the USA,* Charles A. Ferguson and Shirley Brice Heath (New York: Cambridge University Press, 1981), 8.
21. Roseann Duenas Gonzalez, Alice A. Schott, and Victoria F. Vasquez, "The English Language Amendment: Examining Myths," *English Journal,* March 1988, 29.
22. "Say It in English," *Newsweek,* February 20, 1989, 22.
23. Martha Jimenez, spokesperson, Mexican-American Legal Defense and Educational Fund, interview, August 1990.
24. Kathryn Imahara, director of the Language Rights Program, Asian-Pacific American Legal Center, interview, July 1990.
25. Stanley Diamond, spokesperson, U.S. English, interview, August 1990.
26. "Say It in English," 22.
27. Raymond N. Price, "English /in-glish/ n 1a: our official language," *VFW,* 1989.
28. "Spotlight on Antonia Hernandez," *AAUW Outlook* 83, no. 5 (October/November 1989): 8.

CHAPTER FOUR: THE POLITICS OF OFFICIAL ENGLISH LAWS TODAY

1. *U.S. English Update* 8, no. 2 (March/April 1990): 4.
2. Arturo Madrid, "Official English: A False Policy Issue," *The Annals of the American Academy of Political and Social Science* 508 (March 1990): 62.
3. "Spotlight on Antonia Hernandez," *AAUW Outlook* 83, no. 5 (October/November 1989): 9.
4. Jamie B. Draper and Martha Jimenez, "Language Debates in the United States: A Decade in Review," *EPIC Events* 2, no. 5 (November/December 1989): 4–7.
5. "English Plus Initiatives Underway in Several States," *EPIC Events* 2, no. 1 (March/April 1989): 5.
6. Stanley Diamond, spokesperson, U.S. English, interview, August 1990.
7. "The English Language Amendment and Congress: A Chronology of the 1980s," *EPIC Events* 2, no. 5 (November/December, 1989): 5.

8. James Crawford, "Linda Chavez Gives It to Us in Plain English," *EPIC Events* 2, nos. 2–3 (May–August 1989): 9.
9. "English Plus Information Clearinghouse Statement of Purpose," *EPIC Events* 2, no. 1 (March/April 1989): 2–3.
10. Mary Carol Combs, "Official English in 1989: Post Electoral Fallout," *EPIC Events* 2, no. 1 (March/April 1989): 1.
11. Sarah Henry, "Fighting Words," *Los Angeles Times Magazine,* June 10, 1990, 16.
12. Ibid., 18.
13. Kathryn Imahara, director of the Language Rights Program, Asian-Pacific American Legal Center, interview, July 1990.
14. Henry, "Fighting Words," 37.
15. "U.S. English Update File Facts: The Need for Official English Legislation," *U.S. English Update* 8, no. 2 (March/April 1990): 7.
16. Imahara, interview.
17. S. I. Hayakawa, "Ruling on English-Only Law Frustrates Arizona Electorate," for *The New York Times,* printed in the *Oxnard Press-Courier,* February 25, 1990.
18. Henry, "Fighting Words," 16.
19. Mary Carol Combs and Lynn M. Lynch, "English Plus," *English Today* 4, no. 4 (October 1988): 36–42.
20. Imahara, interview.

CHAPTER FIVE: BILINGUAL EDUCATION
PROGRAMS—HOW THEY WORK

1. "A Glossary of Bilingual-Education Terms," *Education Week,* April 1, 1987, 29.
2. "The Special Case of Bilingual Education for Indian Students," *Education Week,* April 1, 1987, 46.
3. Ibid., 44.
4. Agnes Holm and Wayne Holm, "Rock Point, A Navajo Way to Go to School; A Valediction," *The Annals of the American Academy of Political and Social Science* 508, (March 1990): 176–78.
5. Maria Ott, administrative officer of Bilingual/ESL Instruction, Los Angeles Unified School District, interview, August 1990.

6. "Project Aims to Bridge Gap Between Research, Classroom," *Education Week,* April 1, 1987, 43.
7. Maria Ott, interview.
8. Judith Harlan, *Hispanic Voters: A Voice in American Politics* (New York: Franklin Watts, 1988), 43.
9. Sidney H. Morison, "A Spanish-English Dual-Language Program in New York City," *The Annals of the American Academy of Political and Social Science* 508 (March 1990): 160–66.
10. Rosalie Pedalino Porter, "The Newton Alternative to Bilingual Education," *The Annals of the American Academy of Political and Social Science* 508 (March 1990): 150–58.

CHAPTER SIX: THE POLITICS OF
BILINGUAL EDUCATION
1. Michael Quintanilla, "Voices of Experience," *Los Angeles Times,* January 28, 1990, E1.
2. Kenji Hakuta, *Mirror of Language: The Debate on Bilingualism* (New York: Basic Books, 1986), 199.
3. Ibid., 197.
4. James Crawford, "Bilingual Education Traces Its U.S. Roots to the Colonial Era," *Education Week,* April 1, 1987, 22.
5. Hakuta, *Mirror of Language,* 197.
6. James J. Lyons, "The Past and Future Directions of Federal Bilingual-Education Policy," *The Annals of the American Academy of Political and Social Science* 508 (March 1990): 68.
7. Ibid., 68.
8. Walter G. Secada, "Research, Politics, and Bilingual Education," *The Annals of the American Academy of Political and Social Science* 508 (March 1990): 89.
9. Lyons, "Past and Future Directions," 71.
10. Ibid., quoting 94 S.Ct. 786, 788 (1974).
11. Hakuta, *Mirror of Language,* 201.
12. Lyons, "Past and Future Directions," 72.
13. Ibid., 73.
14. Ibid. Quoting from James Crawford, *Bilingual Education: History, Politics, Theory and Practice* (Trenton, N.J.: Crane, 1989).

15. Francis X. Clines, "Reagan Defends Cuts in Budget and Asks for Help of Mayors," *The New York Times,* March 3, 1981, A1.
16. Hakuta, *Mirror of Language,* 208.
17. Ibid., 208–9.
18. *Congressional Digest* 66, no. 3 (March 1987): 71.

CHAPTER SEVEN: LOOKING FOR ANSWERS
1. John Van de Kamp, Willie L. Brown, Jr., Daryl F. Gates, "Argument Against Proposition 63," *California Ballot Pamphlet,* for General Election, November 4, 1986, 47.

Bibliography

Bailyn, Bernard. *The Peopling of British North America: An Introduction.* New York: Knopf, 1986.

"The Balkans, U.S.A." *National Review* 42, no. 4 (March 5, 1990).

Banks, Howard. "Do We Want Quebec Here?" *Forbes,* June 11, 1990.

"Bilingual Education." *Congressional Digest* 66, no. 3 (March 1987).

Boorstin, Daniel J. *The Americans: The National Experience.* New York: Random House, 1965.

Brimelow, Peter. "A Cautionary Case of Bilingualism." *Commentary* 84, no. 5 (November 1987).

Callwood, June. *Portrait of Canada.* Garden City, N.Y.: Doubleday, 1981.

The Canadian Encyclopedia. Vols. 1–3. Edmonton, Canada: Hurtig Publishers, 1985.

Cejas, Paul, Rosa Castro Feinberg, and S. I. Hayakawa. "The English-Only Debate," *Vista,* February 8, 1987.

Francis X. Clines, "Reagan Defends Cuts in Budget and Asks for Help of Mayors." *The New York Times,* March 3, 1981.

Combs, Mary Carol. "Official English in 1989: Post Electoral Fallout." *EPIC Events* no. 1 (March/April 1989).

Combs, Mary Carol, and Lynn M. Lynch. "English Plus." *English Today* 4, no. 4 (October 1988).

Comrie, Bernard, ed. *The World's Major Languages.* New York: Oxford University Press, 1987.

Congressional Digest 66, no. 3 (March 1987).

Conkin, Paul K. *Big Daddy from the Pedernales.* Boston: Twayne Publishers, 1986.

Crawford, James. *Bilingual Education: History, Politics, Theory and Practice.* Trenton, N.J.: Crane, 1989.

————. "Bilingual Education: Language, Learning, and Politics." *Education Week,* April 1, 1987.

Diamond, Stanley. spokesperson, U.S. English, interview, August 1990.

Draper, Jamie B., and Martha Jimenez. "Language Debates in the United States: A Decade in Review." *EPIC Events* 2, no. 5 (November/December 1989).

Einhorn, David, and Stela Ortiz Einhorn. "A Choice of Words." *Americas* 41, no. 1 (January/February 1989).

"The English Language Amendment and Congress: A Chronology of the 1980s." *EPIC Events* 2, no. 5 (November/December 1989).

"English Only: The Threat of Language Restrictions." *NALEO Background Paper Number 10,* 1989.

"English Plus Information Clearinghouse Statement of Purpose." *EPIC Events* 2, no. 1 (March/April 1989).

"English Plus Initiatives Underway in Several States." *EPIC Events* 2, no. 1 (March/April 1989).

Ferguson, Charles A., and Shirley Brice Heath, *Language in the USA.* New York: Cambridge University Press, 1981.

Fulford, Robert. "Canada, A Great Northern Paradox?" *Americas* 42, no. 1 (January/February 1990).

"A Glossary of Bilingual-Education Terms." *Education Week,* April 1, 1987.

Gonzalez, Roseann Duenas, Alice A. Schott, and Victoria F. Vasquez. "The English Language Amendment: Examining Myths." *English Journal,* March 1988.

Graham, Gerald S. *A Concise History of Canada.* New York: The Viking Press, 1968.

Hakuta, Kenji. *Mirror of Language: The Debate on Bilingualism.* New York: Basic Books, 1986.

121

Hargrove, Erwin C. *Jimmy Carter as President.* Baton Rouge and London: Louisiana State University Press, 1988.

Harlan, Judith. *Hispanic Voters: A Voice in American Politics.* New York: Franklin Watts, 1988.

Hawke, David Freeman. *Everyday Life in Early America.* New York: Harper & Row, 1988.

Hayakawa, S. I. "Ruling on English-Only Law Frustrates Arizona Electorate," for *The New York Times,* printed in the *Oxnard Press-Courier,* February 25, 1990.

————. U.S. English press kit, including letter of solicitation, brochures, and flyers, received June 1990.

Heath, Shirley Brice. "English in Our Language Heritage." In *Language in the USA,* Charles A. Ferguson and Shirley Brice Heath. New York: Cambridge University Press 1981.

Henry, Sarah. "Fighting Words." *Los Angeles Times Magazine,* June 10, 1990.

Henry, William A., III. "Beyond the Melting Pot." *Time,* April 9, 1990.

Hoffman, Mark S., ed. *The World Almanac and Book of Facts, 1990.* New York: Pharos Books, 1990.

Holguin, Rick, and George Ramos. "Cultures Follow Separate Paths in Huntington Park." *Los Angeles Times,* April 7, 1990.

Holm, Agnes, and Wayne Holm. "Rock Point, A Navajo Way to Go to School; A Valediction." *The Annals of the American Academy of Political and Social Science* 508 (March 1990).

Hornberger, Nancy H. "Bilingual Education and English-Only: A Language-Planning Framework." *The Annals of the American Academy of Political and Social Science* 508 (March 1990).

Hosch, Harmon M. *Attitudes toward Bilingual Education.* El Paso: Texas Western Press, The University of Texas at El Paso, 1984.

Imahara, Kathryn. Director of the Language Rights Program, Asian-Pacific American Legal Center, interview, July 1990.

Imhoff, Gary. "The Position of U.S. English on Bilingual

Education." *The Annals of the American Academy of Political and Social Science.* 508 (March 1990).

Jiminez, Martha. spokesperson, Mexican-American Legal Defense and Educational Fund, interview, August 1990.

Kjolseth, Rolf. "Cultural Politics of Bilingualism." *Society,* May/June 1983.

Kuralt, Charles. *On the Road with Charles Kuralt.* New York: G. P. Putnam's Sons, 1985.

Leap, William L. "American Indian Languages." In *Language in the USA,* Charles A. Ferguson and Shirley Brice Heath. New York: Cambridge University Press, 1981.

Lewis, E. Glyn. *Bilingualism and Bilingual Education: A Comparative Study.* Albuquerque: University of New Mexico Press, 1980.

Lorant, Stefan. *The Life and Times of Theodore Roosevelt.* Garden City, N.Y.: Doubleday, 1959.

Lyons, James J. "The Past and Future Directions of Federal Bilingual-Education Policy." *The Annals of the American Academy of Political and Social Science* 508 (March 1990).

McCrum, Robert, William Cran, and Robert MacNeil, *The Story of English.* New York: Elisabeth Sifton Books, Viking Penguin, 1986.

McCullough, David Willis. ed. *American Childhoods: An Anthology.* Boston: Little, Brown, 1987.

MacKaye, Susannah D. A. "California Proposition 63: Language Attitudes Reflected in the Public Debate." *The Annals of the American Academy of Political and Social Science* 508 (March 1990).

Madrid, Arturo. "Official English: A False Policy Issue." *The Annals of the American Academy of Political and Social Science* 508 (March 1990).

Marckwardt, Albert H. revision by J. L. Dillard, *American English.* New York: Oxford University Press, 1958, 1980.

Morgan, Thomas. "The Latinization of America." *Esquire,* May 1983.

Morison, Sidney H. "A Spanish-English Dual-Language Program in New York City." *The Annals of the American Academy of Political and Social Science* 508 (March 1990).

Paulston, Christina Bratt. "Bilingualism and Education." In

Language in the USA, Charles A. Ferguson and Shirley Brice Heath. New York: Cambridge University Press, 1981.

―――――. "Understanding Educational Policies in Multilingual States." *The Annals of the American Academy of Political and Social Science* 508 (March 1990).

Paxton, John, ed. *The Statesman's Year-Book.* 125th ed. New York: St. Martin's Press, 1988.

Porter, Rosalie Pedalino. "The Newton Alternative to Bilingual Education." *The Annals of the American Academy of Political and Social Science* 508 (March 1990).

Price, Raymond N. "English /in-glish/ n la: our official language." *VFW,* 1989.

Quinn, David Beers. *The Lost Colonists: Their Fortune and Probable Fate.* Raleigh, N.C.: North Carolina Division of Archives and History, 1984.

Quintanilla, Michael. "Voices of Experience." *Los Angeles Times,* January 28, 1990.

"The Return to Two Solitudes." *Maclean's* 102, no. 45 (November 6, 1989).

Ridge, Martin, ed. *The New Bilingualism: An American Dilemma.* New Brunswick, N.J.: Transaction Books— Rutgers University, 1981.

Rodriguez, Richard. *Hunger of Memory: The Education of Richard Rodriguez.* Boston: David R. Godine, 1981.

"Say It in English." *Newsweek,* February 20, 1989.

Secada, Walter G. "Research, Politics, and Bilingual Education." *The Annals of the American Academy of Political and Social Science* 508 (March 1990).

Sinisi, J. Sebastian. "Official-English Backer Speaks at CU." *The Denver Post,* May 12, 1990.

Sittón, Salomón Nahmad. "The Bilingual Experience in Mexico." In *The New Bilingualism: An American Dilemma,* edited by Martin Ridge, New Brunswick, N.J.: Transaction Books—Rutgers University, 1981.

"Spotlight on Antonia Hernandez," *AAUW Outlook* 83, no. 5 (October/November 1989).

Stalker, James C. "Official English or English Only." *English Journal,* March 1988.

Sundberg, Trudy J. "The Case Against Bilingualism." *English Journal,* March 1988.

Taylor, Greg W. "Uncertain Survival." *Maclean's* 102, no. 45 (November 6, 1989).

Thernstrom, Stephan, ed. *Harvard Encyclopedia of American Ethnic Groups.* Cambridge, Mass.: Belknap Press of Harvard University Press, 1980.

Udall, Stewart L. *To the Inland Empire: Coronado and Our Spanish Legacy.* Garden City, N.Y.: Doubleday, 1987.

U.S. Bureau of the Census. *Statistical Abstract of the United States: 1989* (109th Edition) Washington, D.C., 1989.
————. *U.S.A. Statistics in Brief 1990: A Statistical Abstract Supplement,* Washington, D.C., 1990.

U.S. English Update 8, no. 2 (March/April 1990).

Van de Kamp, John, Willie L. Brown, Jr., Daryl F. Gates. "Argument Against Proposition 63." *California Ballot Pamphlet,* for General Election, November 4, 1986.

Walsh, Mary Williams. "A Tongue Lashing in Canada." *Los Angeles Times,* February 13, 1990.

Weisberger, Bernard A. *The American People.* New York: American Heritage, 1970, 1971.

Williams, Carol J. "In Hungary, Learning Russian Is Out of Style." *Los Angeles Times,* June 15, 1990.

The World Almanac and Book of Facts 1990. New York: Pharos Books, 1990.

Yalden, Maxwell F. "The Bilingual Experience in Canada." In *The New Bilingualism: An American Dilemma,* edited by Martin Ridge. New Brunswick, N.J.: Transaction Books—Rutgers University, 1981.

INDEX